Loyalty Program
Complete Self-Assessment Guide

The guidance in this Self-Assessment is based on Loyalty Program best practices and standards in business process architecture, design and quality management. The guidance is also based on the professional judgment of the individual collaborators listed in the Acknowledgments.

Table of Contents

About The Art of Service

The Art of Service, Business Process Architects since 2000, is dedicated to helping stakeholders achieve excellence.

Defining, designing, creating, and implementing a process to solve a stakeholders challenge or meet an objective is the most valuable role… In EVERY group, company, organization and department.

Unless you're talking a one-time, single-use project, there should be a process. Whether that process is managed and implemented by humans, AI, or a combination of the two, it needs to be designed by someone with a complex enough perspective to ask the right questions.

Someone capable of asking the right questions and step back and say, 'What are we really trying to accomplish here? And is there a different way to look at it?'

With The Art of Service's Standard Requirements Self-Assessments, we empower people who can do just that — whether their title is marketer, entrepreneur, manager, salesperson, consultant, Business Process Manager, executive assistant, IT Manager, CIO etc... —they are the people who rule the future. They are people who watch the process as it happens, and ask the right questions to make the process work better.

Contact us when you need any support with this Self-Assessment and any help with templates, blue-prints and examples of standard documents you might need:

http://theartofservice.com
service@theartofservice.com

Included Resources - how to access

Included with your purchase of the book is the Loyalty Program

Self-Assessment Spreadsheet Dashboard which contains all questions and Self-Assessment areas and auto-generates insights, graphs, and project RACI planning - all with examples to get you started right away.

How? Simply send an email to
access@theartofservice.com
with this books' title in the subject to get the Loyalty Program Self Assessment Tool right away.

You will receive the following contents with New and Updated specific criteria:

•   The latest quick edition of the book in PDF

•   The latest complete edition of the book in PDF, which criteria correspond to the criteria in...

•   The Self-Assessment Excel Dashboard, and...

•   Example pre-filled Self-Assessment Excel Dashboard to get familiar with results generation

•   In-depth specific Checklists covering the topic

•   Project management checklists and templates to assist with implementation

INCLUDES LIFETIME SELF ASSESSMENT UPDATES

Every self assessment comes with Lifetime Updates and Lifetime Free Updated Books. Lifetime Updates is an industry-first feature which allows you to receive verified self assessment updates, ensuring you always have the most accurate information at your fingertips.

Get it now- you will be glad you did - do it now, before you forget.

Send an email to **access@theartofservice.com** with this books' title in the subject to get the Loyalty Program Self Assessment Tool right away.

Purpose of this Self-Assessment

This Self-Assessment has been developed to improve understanding of the requirements and elements of Loyalty Program, based on best practices and standards in business process architecture, design and quality management.

It is designed to allow for a rapid Self-Assessment to determine how closely existing management practices and procedures correspond to the elements of the Self-Assessment.

The criteria of requirements and elements of Loyalty Program have been rephrased in the format of a Self-Assessment questionnaire, with a seven-criterion scoring system, as explained in this document.

In this format, even with limited background knowledge of Loyalty Program, a manager can quickly review existing operations to determine how they measure up to the standards. This in turn can serve as the starting point of a 'gap analysis' to identify management tools or system elements that might usefully be implemented in the organization to help improve overall performance.

How to use the Self-Assessment

On the following pages are a series of questions to identify to what extent your Loyalty Program initiative is complete in comparison to the requirements set in standards.

To facilitate answering the questions, there is a space in front of each question to enter a score on a scale of '1' to '5'.

1 Strongly Disagree

2 Disagree

3 Neutral

4 Agree

5 Strongly Agree

Read the question and rate it with the following in front of mind:

'In my belief, the answer to this question is clearly defined'.

There are two ways in which you can choose to interpret this statement;
1. how aware are you that the answer to the question is clearly defined
2. for more in-depth analysis you can choose to gather evidence and confirm the answer to the question. This obviously will take more time, most Self-Assessment users opt for the first way to interpret the question and dig deeper later on based on the outcome of the overall Self-Assessment.

A score of '1' would mean that the answer is not clear at all, where a '5' would mean the answer is crystal clear and defined. Leave emtpy when the question is not applicable or you don't want to answer it, you can skip it without affecting your score. Write your score in the space provided.

After you have responded to all the appropriate statements in each section, compute your average score for that section, using the formula provided, and round to the nearest tenth. Then transfer to the corresponding spoke in the Loyalty Program Scorecard on the second next page of the Self-Assessment.

Your completed Loyalty Program Scorecard will give you a clear presentation of which Loyalty Program areas need attention.

Loyalty Program
Scorecard Example

Example of how the finalized Scorecard can look like:

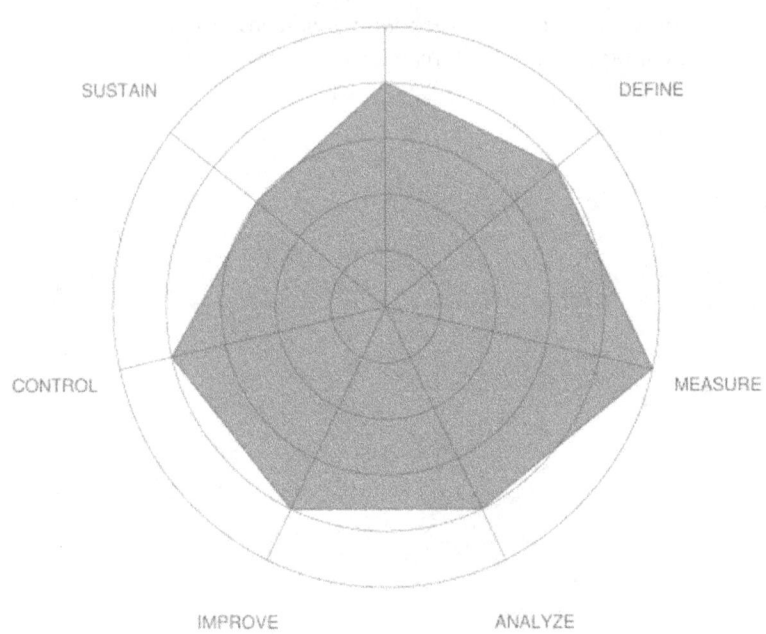

Loyalty Program
Scorecard

Your Scores:

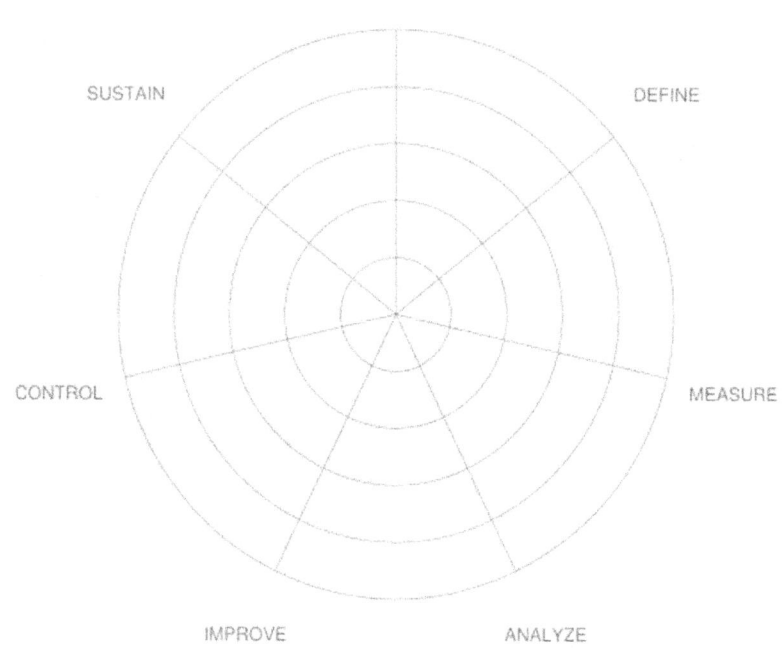

BEGINNING OF THE SELF-ASSESSMENT:

CRITERION #1: RECOGNIZE

INTENT: Be aware of the need for change. Recognize that there is an unfavorable variation, problem or symptom.

In my belief, the answer to this question is clearly defined:

5 Strongly Agree

4 Agree

3 Neutral

2 Disagree

1 Strongly Disagree

1. What are your program teams existing and needed core competencies?
<--- Score

2. Will the needs of this group also satisfy the needs of your top customers?
<--- Score

3. As a sponsor, customer or management, how

important is it to meet goals, objectives?
<--- Score

4. Are there any specific expectations or concerns about the Loyalty Program team, Loyalty Program itself?
<--- Score

5. How should a promised good or service be identified?
<--- Score

6. What do you think you need to know more about in order to use digital tools more effectively?
<--- Score

7. How much are sponsors, customers, partners, stakeholders involved in Loyalty Program? In other words, what are the risks, if Loyalty Program does not deliver successfully?
<--- Score

8. Do you really need a loyalty program?
<--- Score

9. What does Loyalty Program success mean to the stakeholders?
<--- Score

10. What kinds of training are needed?
<--- Score

11. Why do you need a Customer Loyalty Program?
<--- Score

12. How much brand recognition do you have in the market, and what type of brand positioning do you promote?
<--- Score

13. Is this a problem that the customer really needs to be solved?
<--- Score

14. What do customers need and want?
<--- Score

15. What customer needs will it satisfy?
<--- Score

16. Who else hopes to benefit from it?
<--- Score

17. What customer needs are being overlooked in this scenario?
<--- Score

18. How are you going to measure success?
<--- Score

19. What problems are you facing and how do you consider Loyalty Program will circumvent those obstacles?
<--- Score

20. What are the stakeholder objectives to be achieved with Loyalty Program?
<--- Score

21. Can management identify its loyal segments through means other than repeat purchase

patterns?

<--- Score

22. What situation(s) led to this Loyalty Program Self Assessment?

<--- Score

23. What volunteer skills and experiences do you need to make your program successful?

<--- Score

24. How are the Loyalty Program's objectives aligned to the group's overall stakeholder strategy?

<--- Score

25. Is adherence a relevant issue in the self-management education of diabetes?

<--- Score

26. Who are potential customers that have the problem your product solves?

<--- Score

27. What other organizations do you know of that have taken a position on issues associated with marketing and advertising in organizations?

<--- Score

28. What are the expected benefits of Loyalty Program to the stakeholder?

<--- Score

29. Do you see customer dissatisfaction with limited award seat availability as an issue that will continue to plague the modern loyalty program?

<--- Score

30. What main problems does a provider identify in the introduction of Cloud to the business customer?

<--- Score

31. Do you earn the Builder Bonus with your current structure or do you need to enroll new members?

<--- Score

32. What would happen if Loyalty Program weren't done?

<--- Score

33. Do you or your customers need a loyalty scheme?

<--- Score

34. How should entity A recognize revenue for this arrangement?

<--- Score

Add up total points for this section:
_ _ _ _ _ = Total points for this section

Divided by: _ _ _ _ _ _ (number of statements answered) = _ _ _ _ _ _
Average score for this section

Transfer your score to the Loyalty Program Index at the beginning of the Self-Assessment.

CRITERION #2: DEFINE:

INTENT: Formulate the stakeholder problem. Define the problem, needs and objectives.

In my belief, the answer to this question is clearly defined:

5 Strongly Agree

4 Agree

3 Neutral

2 Disagree

1 Strongly Disagree

1. Has everyone on the team, including the team leaders, been properly trained?
<--- Score

2. Are team charters developed?
<--- Score

3. Is there a critical path to deliver Loyalty Program results?

<--- Score

4. What are the compelling stakeholder reasons for embarking on Loyalty Program?
<--- Score

5. Will team members regularly document their Loyalty Program work?
<--- Score

6. Is full participation by members in regularly held team meetings guaranteed?
<--- Score

7. Is the team equipped with available and reliable resources?
<--- Score

8. Are there any constraints known that bear on the ability to perform Loyalty Program work? How is the team addressing them?
<--- Score

9. Have the customer needs been translated into specific, measurable requirements? How?
<--- Score

10. Has the direction changed at all during the course of Loyalty Program? If so, when did it change and why?
<--- Score

11. How was the 'as is' process map developed, reviewed, verified and validated?
<--- Score

12. Who are the Loyalty Program improvement team members, including Management Leads and Coaches?
<--- Score

13. Are different versions of process maps needed to account for the different types of inputs?
<--- Score

14. What are the Roles and Responsibilities for each team member and its leadership? Where is this documented?
<--- Score

15. How does the Loyalty Program manager ensure against scope creep?
<--- Score

16. Has anyone else (internal or external to the group) attempted to solve this problem or a similar one before? If so, what knowledge can be leveraged from these previous efforts?
<--- Score

17. How will variation in the actual durations of each activity be dealt with to ensure that the expected Loyalty Program results are met?
<--- Score

18. Is Loyalty Program linked to key stakeholder goals and objectives?
<--- Score

19. What specifically is the problem? Where does it occur? When does it occur? What is its extent?
<--- Score

20. Is there a completed SIPOC representation, describing the Suppliers, Inputs, Process, Outputs, and Customers?
<--- Score

21. What difficulties did it encounter in the implementation of services in the similar case?
<--- Score

22. Do the procedures contain provisions for review and update of training requirements?
<--- Score

23. When is/was the Loyalty Program start date?
<--- Score

24. Is there regularly 100% attendance at the team meetings? If not, have appointed substitutes attended to preserve cross-functionality and full representation?
<--- Score

25. Is data collected and displayed to better understand customer(s) critical needs and requirements.
<--- Score

26. Is there a completed, verified, and validated high-level 'as is' (not 'should be' or 'could be') stakeholder process map?
<--- Score

27. Has a project plan, Gantt chart, or similar been developed/completed?
<--- Score

28. What would be the goal or target for a Loyalty Program's improvement team?
<--- Score

29. Have you a service strategy clearly defined in terms of customer benefits?
<--- Score

30. Does your organization have a relationship with one or more third-party agents (for example, gateways, web-hosting companies, airline booking agents, loyalty program agents, etc.)?
<--- Score

31. Is the team formed and are team leaders (Coaches and Management Leads) assigned?
<--- Score

32. Is the current 'as is' process being followed? If not, what are the discrepancies?
<--- Score

33. Is the team sponsored by a champion or stakeholder leader?
<--- Score

34. Has a team charter been developed and communicated?
<--- Score

35. Does your organization have a relationship with one or more third-party service providers (for example, gateways, web-hosting companies, airline booking agents, loyalty program agents, etc)?

<--- Score

36. Do the problem and goal statements meet the SMART criteria (specific, measurable, attainable, relevant, and time-bound)?
<--- Score

37. How do you keep key subject matter experts in the loop?
<--- Score

38. What are the dynamics of the communication plan?
<--- Score

39. Does the team have regular meetings?
<--- Score

40. Are improvement team members fully trained on Loyalty Program?
<--- Score

41. If substitutes have been appointed, have they been briefed on the Loyalty Program goals and received regular communications as to the progress to date?
<--- Score

42. How does this organization meet all your requirements and expectations?
<--- Score

43. Does your organization require merchant applications to be in writing?
<--- Score

44. How do you showcase and communicate your social media success?
<--- Score

45. Has the Loyalty Program work been fairly and/ or equitably divided and delegated among team members who are qualified and capable to perform the work? Has everyone contributed?
<--- Score

46. What customer feedback methods were used to solicit their input?
<--- Score

47. Are stakeholder processes mapped?
<--- Score

48. Has the improvement team collected the 'voice of the customer' (obtained feedback – qualitative and quantitative)?
<--- Score

49. Are customers identified and high impact areas defined?
<--- Score

50. When is the estimated completion date?
<--- Score

51. Is Loyalty Program currently on schedule according to the plan?
<--- Score

52. What constraints exist that might impact the team?
<--- Score

53. Will team members perform Loyalty Program work when assigned and in a timely fashion?
<--- Score

54. What are the rough order estimates on cost savings/opportunities that Loyalty Program brings?
<--- Score

55. How often are the team meetings?
<--- Score

56. When are meeting minutes sent out? Who is on the distribution list?
<--- Score

57. Are there different segments of customers?
<--- Score

58. What are the boundaries of the scope? What is in bounds and what is not? What is the start point? What is the stop point?
<--- Score

59. How will your organization determine if you have fulfilled all requirements?
<--- Score

60. What are the age requirements for participants?
<--- Score

61. How will the Loyalty Program team and the group measure complete success of Loyalty Program?
<--- Score

62. Has a high-level 'as is' process map been completed, verified and validated?
<--- Score

63. Has/have the customer(s) been identified?
<--- Score

64. Is there a Loyalty Program management charter, including stakeholder case, problem and goal statements, scope, milestones, roles and responsibilities, communication plan?
<--- Score

65. How did the Loyalty Program manager receive input to the development of a Loyalty Program improvement plan and the estimated completion dates/times of each activity?
<--- Score

66. Are customer(s) identified and segmented according to their different needs and requirements?
<--- Score

67. What is required to support your loyalty program?
<--- Score

68. Are there tactics being employed by loyalty programs that are concerning enough to require a statutory remedy, regulation, or other intervention as an industry code of conduct?
<--- Score

69. Is the improvement team aware of the different versions of a process: what they think it is vs. what it actually is vs. what it should be vs. what it could be?

<--- Score

70. Is the team adequately staffed with the desired cross-functionality? If not, what additional resources are available to the team?
<--- Score

71. What critical content must be communicated – who, what, when, where, and how?
<--- Score

72. Is the Loyalty Program scope manageable?
<--- Score

73. What is required at your end to create a loyalty program?
<--- Score

74. What key stakeholder process output measure(s) does Loyalty Program leverage and how?
<--- Score

75. Is a fully trained team formed, supported, and committed to work on the Loyalty Program improvements?
<--- Score

76. How would you define customer satisfaction?
<--- Score

77. How is the team tracking and documenting its work?
<--- Score

Add up total points for this section:
_ _ _ _ _ = Total points for this section

Divided by: _ _ _ _ _ _ (number of
statements answered) = _ _ _ _ _ _
Average score for this section

Transfer your score to the Loyalty
Program Index at the beginning of the
Self-Assessment.

CRITERION #3: MEASURE:

In my belief, the answer to this question is clearly defined:

5 Strongly Agree

4 Agree

3 Neutral

2 Disagree

1 Strongly Disagree

1. What data was collected (past, present, future/ongoing)?
<--- Score

2. What do clients want in terms of features, functionallty and cost?
<--- Score

3. How to measure the success of social media

efforts?
<--- Score

4. Is the need to service large numbers of members driving up running costs?
<--- Score

5. Was a data collection plan established?
<--- Score

6. How do you measure engagement?
<--- Score

7. In general, will the program focus on the most profitable customers?
<--- Score

8. What are the key input variables? What are the key process variables? What are the key output variables?
<--- Score

9. What impact does globalization have on corporate responsibility?
<--- Score

10. Are there quantifiable benefits to passive loyalty, as word of mouth and recommendations?
<--- Score

11. How can analyzing retail data help your retail business?
<--- Score

12. Who participated in the data collection for measurements?
<--- Score

13. Are process variation components displayed/ communicated using suitable charts, graphs, plots?
<--- Score

14. Are there true switching costs if a member wants to leave your program?
<--- Score

15. What is the focus of your organization?
<--- Score

16. Can rewards be offered at a reasonable cost?
<--- Score

17. Can the customer data be analyzed in useful ways?
<--- Score

18. Is long term and short term variability accounted for?
<--- Score

19. Is data collection planned and executed?
<--- Score

20. Where to put the analytics team?
<--- Score

21. What is the basis for your organizations data analysis?
<--- Score

22. What is the business value in being customer-focused?
<--- Score

23. What types of statistical analysis will be required?
<--- Score

24. What was the impact of this on share of category requirements met by a particular alliance?
<--- Score

25. What key measures identified indicate the performance of the stakeholder process?
<--- Score

26. What are the possibilities of the data migration and how much does it cost?
<--- Score

27. Is there an impact of customer loyalty programs on customer retention?
<--- Score

28. How does your loyalty program impact brand affinity?
<--- Score

29. How did your office visit impact you?
<--- Score

30. How do you measure the effectiveness of your marketing activities?
<--- Score

31. How do consumers currently view role in a loyalty program, and to what extent do perceptions impact evaluations of the program?

<--- Score

32. Are the sales and cost data reliable?
<--- Score

33. How has the formation of global alliances affected the perceptions of business travelers to switching costs?
<--- Score

34. How does your pipeline and mix impact your bottom line in cash?
<--- Score

35. Does the academic level and gender of the employees impact the relationship between services and external factors?
<--- Score

36. Is data collected on key measures that were identified?
<--- Score

37. What are the potential benefits of data analysis?
<--- Score

38. What has the team done to assure the stability and accuracy of the measurement process?
<--- Score

39. What are the agreed upon definitions of the high impact areas, defect(s), unit(s), and opportunities that will figure into the process capability metrics?
<--- Score

40. How does your organization achieve cost effectiveness in operating loyalty programs?
<--- Score

41. Have you found any 'ground fruit' or 'low-hanging fruit' for immediate remedies to the gap in performance?
<--- Score

42. What switching costs work for customer retention?
<--- Score

43. What does a good business impact analysis look like?
<--- Score

44. What charts has the team used to display the components of variation in the process?
<--- Score

45. How do you aggregate & analyze the data to actually improve customer satisfaction & quality?
<--- Score

46. How much does your loyalty program, and associated marketing efforts, cost?
<--- Score

47. Do you quantify the value of a loyalty program?
<--- Score

48. Is the data collected and analyzed based on customer segments or products?
<--- Score

49. Do you have a way to measure the incremental sales the program generates?

<--- Score

50. Are high impact defects defined and identified in the stakeholder process?

<--- Score

51. How large is the gap between current performance and the customer-specified (goal) performance?

<--- Score

52. Is there an impact of customer retention?

<--- Score

53. Is Process Variation Displayed/Communicated?

<--- Score

54. Should your technology spend be focused on sales building or expense control?

<--- Score

55. Are marketing strategies developed with a focus on increasing volume of purchases (for example loyalty programs)?

<--- Score

56. Is there a Performance Baseline?

<--- Score

57. Are key measures identified and agreed upon?

<--- Score

58. How did your commercial impact sales?

<--- Score

59. How does competition impact the form of the optimal linear loyalty program?
<--- Score

60. Is key measure data collection planned and executed, process variation displayed and communicated and performance baselined?
<--- Score

61. How where the successes of the program measured in reference to the outcomes to the original key objectives?
<--- Score

62. How does competition impact the optimal sign-up bonus?
<--- Score

63. What is the status of measurements/KPIs that track loyalty efforts now, by end of year and within 18 months?
<--- Score

64. How do you put migration analysis to work in order to create profits from your database and improve customer relationships?
<--- Score

65. Is a solid data collection plan established that includes measurement systems analysis?
<--- Score

66. What particular quality tools did the team find helpful in establishing measurements?

<--- Score

67. Do you measure the ROI of your social media marketing?

<--- Score

Add up total points for this section:
_____ = Total points for this section

Divided by: _____ (number of statements answered) = _____
Average score for this section

Transfer your score to the Loyalty Program Index at the beginning of the Self-Assessment.

CRITERION #4: ANALYZE:

INTENT: Analyze causes, assumptions and hypotheses.

In my belief, the answer to this question is clearly defined:

5 Strongly Agree

4 Agree

3 Neutral

2 Disagree

1 Strongly Disagree

1. Is the gap/opportunity displayed and communicated in financial terms?
<--- Score

2. What quality tools were used to get through the analyze phase?
<--- Score

3. Were there any improvement opportunities identified from the process analysis?

<--- Score

4. Where can customers seek further information on how data will be stored and used?
<--- Score

5. What if the customer data needed is not part of a companies original collected dataset?
<--- Score

6. What are the revised rough estimates of the financial savings/opportunity for Loyalty Program improvements?
<--- Score

7. Is a quick service mode available?
<--- Score

8. Was a detailed process map created to amplify critical steps of the 'as is' stakeholder process?
<--- Score

9. How was the detailed process map generated, verified, and validated?
<--- Score

10. What did the team gain from developing a sub-process map?
<--- Score

11. What were the crucial 'moments of truth' on the process map?
<--- Score

12. What conclusions were drawn from the team's data collection and analysis? How did the team reach

these conclusions?
<--- Score

13. Which best describes the resources used to improve marketing data quality?
<--- Score

14. How do you automate the different process steps in your loyalty program?
<--- Score

15. What kinds of customer data are being generated through loyalty programs?
<--- Score

16. Who will have access to your data?
<--- Score

17. Who are your most valuable customers and how do you extract more value out of your customer database?
<--- Score

18. Is the performance gap determined?
<--- Score

19. What tools were used to generate the list of possible causes?
<--- Score

20. Are you a provider looking for your next opportunity?
<--- Score

21. What is the cost of poor quality as supported by the team's analysis?

<--- Score

22. How do you get the customer to give you this data?
<--- Score

23. What drives consumer participation to loyalty programs?
<--- Score

24. Do you have enough customer data?
<--- Score

25. Is data and process analysis, root cause analysis and quantifying the gap/opportunity in place?
<--- Score

26. Are gaps between current performance and the goal performance identified?
<--- Score

27. Which credit card processor is best?
<--- Score

28. What were the financial benefits resulting from any 'ground fruit or low-hanging fruit' (quick fixes)?
<--- Score

29. How do you ensure that research organizations provide you with quality data?
<--- Score

30. What does the data say about the performance of the stakeholder process?
<--- Score

31. Did any value-added analysis or 'lean thinking' take place to identify some of the gaps shown on the 'as is' process map?
<--- Score

32. What are the strengths, weaknesses, opportunities and threats facing your Program?
<--- Score

33. How are you establishing a loyalty card database for storing the unique card identies?
<--- Score

34. How do you run a sales report on sales done at the quick serve terminal(s)?
<--- Score

35. Is the Loyalty Program process severely broken such that a re-design is necessary?
<--- Score

36. What are you doing with your customer and loyalty data?
<--- Score

37. How do you use digital technology and what you know about members to create unique experiences that drive business?
<--- Score

38. Were any designed experiments used to generate additional insight into the data analysis?
<--- Score

39. What should small businesses be doing to protect customers data?

<--- Score

40. How could technology better facilitate database management in loyalty programs?
<--- Score

41. How do you advance from databases, spreadsheets and dashboards to driving results for businesses and becoming consultants to management?
<--- Score

42. How do you use loyalty membership data to determine consumer trends?
<--- Score

43. What opportunities exist to improve the internal running of your retail business?
<--- Score

44. How do you put data to work in your store?
<--- Score

45. What tools were used to narrow the list of possible causes?
<--- Score

46. Have any additional benefits been identified that will result from closing all or most of the gaps?
<--- Score

47. How can one accelerate his point earning process?
<--- Score

48. How can you link offline loyalty program

customer data to corresponding online data?
<--- Score

49. Does your organization use the loyalty program data in efforts to predict future trends?
<--- Score

50. Were Pareto charts (or similar) used to portray the 'heavy hitters' (or key sources of variation)?
<--- Score

51. Did any additional data need to be collected?
<--- Score

52. Is social media really the most engaging channel or are marketers seduced by data?
<--- Score

53. What are the most effective tactics used to improve marketing data quality?
<--- Score

54. Which are the most influential drivers of satisfaction?
<--- Score

55. How do you use loyalty membership usage history data to reduce consumer defections?
<--- Score

56. Do incentive models have to be financially driven?
<--- Score

57. Have the problem and goal statements been updated to reflect the additional knowledge gained

from the analyze phase?
<--- Score

58. Which are typically included in your organizations sales onboarding process?
<--- Score

59. Do you have access to your customer database?
<--- Score

60. Was a cause-and-effect diagram used to explore the different types of causes (or sources of variation)?
<--- Score

Add up total points for this section:
_____ = Total points for this section

Divided by: _____ (number of statements answered) = _____
Average score for this section

Transfer your score to the Loyalty Program Index at the beginning of the Self-Assessment.

CRITERION #5: IMPROVE:

INTENT: Develop a practical solution. Innovate, establish and test the solution and to measure the results.

In my belief, the answer to this question is clearly defined:

5 Strongly Agree

4 Agree

3 Neutral

2 Disagree

1 Strongly Disagree

1. How will the group know that the solution worked?
<--- Score

2. What tools were used to evaluate the potential solutions?
<--- Score

3. What does the 'should be' process map/design look like?

<--- Score

4. Does consumer loyalty as a result of gamification differ by gender?
<--- Score

5. What were the underlying assumptions on the cost-benefit analysis?
<--- Score

6. Are there any constraints (technical, political, cultural, or otherwise) that would inhibit certain solutions?
<--- Score

7. Is a solution implementation plan established, including schedule/work breakdown structure, resources, risk management plan, cost/budget, and control plan?
<--- Score

8. Was a pilot designed for the proposed solution(s)?
<--- Score

9. How do competitors develop and manage customer loyalty programs?
<--- Score

10. What tools were used to tap into the creativity and encourage 'outside the box' thinking?
<--- Score

11. Are possible solutions generated and tested?
<--- Score

12. Under what conditions will a loyalty rewards

program have a positive effect on customer evaluations, behavior, and repatronage intentions?
<--- Score

13. Do you think that your Program is improving Members loyalty to your brand?
<--- Score

14. How will the team or the process owner(s) monitor the implementation plan to see that it is working as intended?
<--- Score

15. What is the optimal design of program structure?
<--- Score

16. Is it easy to understand how the rewards program works?
<--- Score

17. What makes a guest decide to join a loyalty program?
<--- Score

18. Is a contingency plan established?
<--- Score

19. Is the implementation plan designed?
<--- Score

20. What lessons, if any, from a pilot were incorporated into the design of the full-scale solution?
<--- Score

21. What type of solution(s) does your organization use to manage loyalty marketing functions and services?
<--- Score

22. What are the activities related to the development and / or adjustment of your loyalty program?
<--- Score

23. What types of products are evaluated?
<--- Score

24. What tools were most useful during the improve phase?
<--- Score

25. How does your organization decide if loyalty is an appropriate objective of customer loyalty program?
<--- Score

26. What error proofing will be done to address some of the discrepancies observed in the 'as is' process?
<--- Score

27. What is the team's contingency plan for potential problems occurring in implementation?
<--- Score

28. Does industry structure play a role in loyalty development among its members?
<--- Score

29. Do you reward people for performance improvement and excellence?

<--- Score

30. Have the results been reported to top management?
<--- Score

31. How do other organizations decide the budget for loyalty program marketing spending?
<--- Score

32. How does balanced scorecard help your managers develop social and environmental goals and objectives?
<--- Score

33. Is there a small-scale pilot for proposed improvement(s)? What conclusions were drawn from the outcomes of a pilot?
<--- Score

34. Can program benefits be delivered to the person making the purchase decision?
<--- Score

35. Is there a cost/benefit analysis of optimal solution(s)?
<--- Score

36. Is pilot data collected and analyzed?
<--- Score

37. How did the team generate the list of possible solutions?
<--- Score

38. Do you cooperate with your manufacturers to

improve your customer loyalty program?
<--- Score

39. Why do some payment solutions succeed, while others fail?
<--- Score

40. Does the documentation system show that the audit results are communicated to management?
<--- Score

41. Does the advertisement influence on customer purchase decision?
<--- Score

42. Were any criteria developed to assist the team in testing and evaluating potential solutions?
<--- Score

43. What communications are necessary to support the implementation of the solution?
<--- Score

44. Are improved process ('should be') maps modified based on pilot data and analysis?
<--- Score

45. Are the best solutions selected?
<--- Score

46. How does the solution remove the key sources of issues discovered in the analyze phase?
<--- Score

47. What makes pls rewards different from any other loyalty solution in the market today?

<--- Score

48. What alternatives does a service provider have to help improve corresponding situations?
<--- Score

49. Are new and improved process ('should be') maps developed?
<--- Score

50. What is the implementation plan?
<--- Score

51. What attendant changes will need to be made to ensure that the solution is successful?
<--- Score

52. Describe the design of the pilot and what tests were conducted, if any?
<--- Score

53. How does your loyalty program improve the average lifetime value of your customers?
<--- Score

54. Does loyalty program influence the purchasing decision?
<--- Score

55. Do members understand the value of your loyalty program?
<--- Score

56. How do other organizations approach the setup and development of an online loyalty program?

<--- Score

57. What is Loyalty Program's impact on utilizing the best solution(s)?
<--- Score

58. Does the customer understand the trend?
<--- Score

59. Is the optimal solution selected based on testing and analysis?
<--- Score

Add up total points for this section:
_____ = Total points for this section

Divided by: _____ (number of statements answered) = _____
Average score for this section

Transfer your score to the Loyalty Program Index at the beginning of the Self-Assessment.

CRITERION #6: CONTROL:

INTENT: Implement the practical solution. Maintain the performance and correct possible complications.

In my belief, the answer to this question is clearly defined:

5 Strongly Agree

4 Agree

3 Neutral

2 Disagree

1 Strongly Disagree

1. Does the Loyalty Program performance meet the customer's requirements?
<--- Score

2. Does the response plan contain a definite closed loop continual improvement scheme (e.g., plan-do-check-act)?
<--- Score

3. Have new or revised work instructions resulted?
<--- Score

4. Is there a recommended audit plan for routine surveillance inspections of Loyalty Program's gains?
<--- Score

5. What performance standards must the program live up to?
<--- Score

6. Is a response plan in place for when the input, process, or output measures indicate an 'out-of-control' condition?
<--- Score

7. What key inputs and outputs are being measured on an ongoing basis?
<--- Score

8. What is the control/monitoring plan?
<--- Score

9. How does your organization plan to improve the customer experience as it relates to customer communications?
<--- Score

10. How will the process owner and team be able to hold the gains?
<--- Score

11. What is the single most important deciding factor when you plan a vacation?
<--- Score

12. Are operating procedures consistent?
<--- Score

13. How many staff do you plan to employ?
<--- Score

14. How frequently is the plan is tested or updated?
<--- Score

15. How will the day-to-day responsibilities for monitoring and continual improvement be transferred from the improvement team to the process owner?
<--- Score

16. Is there a transfer of ownership and knowledge to process owner and process team tasked with the responsibilities.
<--- Score

17. Are documented procedures clear and easy to follow for the operators?
<--- Score

18. What quality tools were useful in the control phase?
<--- Score

19. Where are you planning to invest within loyalty marketing?
<--- Score

20. Is new knowledge gained imbedded in the response plan?
<--- Score

21. Are new process steps, standards, and documentation ingrained into normal operations?
<--- Score

22. Is there a standardized process?
<--- Score

23. What are your plans for improving the work climate in your area?
<--- Score

24. How will input, process, and output variables be checked to detect for sub-optimal conditions?
<--- Score

25. Is a response plan established and deployed?
<--- Score

26. Where do you learn the most about loyalty programs?
<--- Score

27. Are suggested corrective/restorative actions indicated on the response plan for known causes to problems that might surface?
<--- Score

28. Are there documented procedures?
<--- Score

29. Will any special training be provided for results interpretation?
<--- Score

30. Is there documentation that will support the

successful operation of the improvement?
<--- Score

31. What happens when mobile users actually click-through your site to learn more about your business?
<--- Score

32. What is the recommended frequency of auditing?
<--- Score

33. How will the process owner verify improvement in present and future sigma levels, process capabilities?
<--- Score

34. How might the group capture best practices and lessons learned so as to leverage improvements?
<--- Score

35. What other systems, operations, processes, and infrastructures (hiring practices, staffing, training, incentives/rewards, metrics/dashboards/scorecards, etc.) need updates, additions, changes, or deletions in order to facilitate knowledge transfer and improvements?
<--- Score

36. Which part of the resources you want to control directly, and which you can indirectly?
<--- Score

37. Does job training on the documented procedures need to be part of the process team's education and training?
<--- Score

38. What should the next improvement project be that is related to Loyalty Program?
<--- Score

39. What are the critical parameters to watch?
<--- Score

40. Is reporting being used or needed?
<--- Score

41. How will report readings be checked to effectively monitor performance?
<--- Score

42. Is there a control plan in place for sustaining improvements (short and long-term)?
<--- Score

43. How do actual sales this period compare to the current plan?
<--- Score

44. What do you learn from other successful customer loyalty programs?
<--- Score

45. Is knowledge gained on process shared and institutionalized?
<--- Score

46. What has t-mobile learned about social media that other companies could emulate?
<--- Score

47. Have you measurable quality standards for all the service areas?

<--- Score

48. When planning any successful marketing campaign, you need to consider key metrics for success. Did your ad campaign drive awareness for your brand?
<--- Score

49. What is the number one complaint from your customer feedback system and can this be addressed with the planned loyalty program?
<--- Score

50. What is happened in the last couple of years that is made Machine Learning such a potent weapon?
<--- Score

51. What should this plan accomplish?
<--- Score

52. What other areas of the group might benefit from the Loyalty Program team's improvements, knowledge, and learning?
<--- Score

53. Has the improved process and its steps been standardized?
<--- Score

54. What do you learn from loyalty programs that have failed?
<--- Score

55. Does a troubleshooting guide exist or is it needed?
<--- Score

56. Is there a documented and implemented monitoring plan?
<--- Score

57. How will new or emerging customer needs/ requirements be checked/communicated to orient the process toward meeting the new specifications and continually reducing variation?
<--- Score

58. Who is the Loyalty Program process owner?
<--- Score

Add up total points for this section:
_____ = Total points for this section

Divided by: _____ (number of statements answered) = _____
Average score for this section

Transfer your score to the Loyalty Program Index at the beginning of the Self-Assessment.

CRITERION #7: SUSTAIN:

INTENT: Retain the benefits.

In my belief, the answer to this question is clearly defined:

5 Strongly Agree

4 Agree

3 Neutral

2 Disagree

1 Strongly Disagree

1. What rewards do guests most value in a restaurant loyalty program?
<--- Score

2. Sharing economy or access economy?
<--- Score

3. How well do you know the purchase history of your loyal customers?
<--- Score

4. Does this translate into increased customer engagement?
<--- Score

5. What do you see as the responsibilities of the pre-commitment provider?
<--- Score

6. Who is eligible for the loyalty program?
<--- Score

7. Do you have dedicated resources for your loyalty programs?
<--- Score

8. Will there be a currency of the program?
<--- Score

9. What kind of program does your staff effectively execute?
<--- Score

10. What are the potential benefits to customers?
<--- Score

11. Do employer branding loyalty programs really work?
<--- Score

12. How likely is the customer to shift some of his business away from your organization in the future?
<--- Score

13. What is your take on the role that theatrical windows play in your industry?

<--- Score

14. Do you have a direct relationship with your end customers?
<--- Score

15. How does your organization constantly engage customers in the loyalty program?
<--- Score

16. Do loyalty programs offer seamless cross-channel rewards redemption?
<--- Score

17. Why was the loyalty program introduced?
<--- Score

18. Do vip programs always work well?
<--- Score

19. Do you see dependencies across functional areas?
<--- Score

20. What are the benefits of the loyalty bonus programs?
<--- Score

21. What does your customer rewards program look like?
<--- Score

22. Does the name/logo reinforce or at least hint at the nature of the program or its offering?
<--- Score

23. What written information is available for customers and where is it located?
<--- Score

24. What does a good story look like in a brand setting?
<--- Score

25. How do web using customers become significant in retention?
<--- Score

26. Does your organization share any information gathered from the online loyalty program with suppliers?
<--- Score

27. What makes the program effective?
<--- Score

28. Is all the cross merchandising in the store relevant to your customers?
<--- Score

29. How do you earn bonus points?
<--- Score

30. When almost every business has a customer loyalty program, is it really that effective?
<--- Score

31. What it takes to implement social loyalty?
<--- Score

32. How large a share of your members are profitable?

<--- Score

33. Does the person reviewing merchant applications have credit experience?
<--- Score

34. What is the typology of loyalty program value?
<--- Score

35. Which social media outlet has been the most effective when speaking to consumers?
<--- Score

36. Should customers pay for joining loyalty clubs?
<--- Score

37. Are your systems and procedures always aimed at the customer?
<--- Score

38. Which social media sites do you visit and how often do you visit them?
<--- Score

39. When should stock levels be decreased?
<--- Score

40. Does your customer loyalty program increase your market share?
<--- Score

41. What information, if any, does it include about the local area/community?
<--- Score

42. Is your customer loyalty program in need of a

major overhaul?

<--- Score

43. How is your loyalty program different than your competitors?

<--- Score

44. How does a brand tell which group of customers increased engagement is coming from?

<--- Score

45. When do rewards have enhancement effects?

<--- Score

46. How do you technology has changed loyalty marketing?

<--- Score

47. How recently did the customer purchase?

<--- Score

48. What motivates you to shop with a certain business?

<--- Score

49. Who is your target customer?

<--- Score

50. What are the strengths of your product or service value proposition?

<--- Score

51. How many retail loyalty programs do you belong to?

<--- Score

52. What is the tiered Loyalty Program for Associates?

<--- Score

53. Does your customer loyalty program increase the number of your customers?

<--- Score

54. Or should you scratch the program completely?

<--- Score

55. How to attract, win and retain customers?

<--- Score

56. What benefits matter most to consumers with respect to retail loyalty?

<--- Score

57. Who will be involved in this project?

<--- Score

58. Does the staffing keep pace with the volume of merchant applications received daily?

<--- Score

59. Does your organization have some sort of physical loyalty program card?

<--- Score

60. Who are your most profitable customers?

<--- Score

61. How are your products selling across various customer demographics?

<--- Score

62. What does it take to engage your customers?
<--- Score

63. What are the advantages of a Balanced Scorecard?
<--- Score

64. Do you have enough team members to service customers properly?
<--- Score

65. Does your organization promote interaction between customers on it?
<--- Score

66. How do you encourage small business owners to make this transition?
<--- Score

67. What is your loyalty/retention rate?
<--- Score

68. Is social media and social marketing the same?
<--- Score

69. Do your clientele love to visit your store and interact with your team?
<--- Score

70. What are the greatest challenges facing your customer loyalty program/ incentive today?
<--- Score

71. What promotional strategies has your loyalty program used?
<--- Score

72. Are you a member of a loyalty program that you rarely participate in?
<--- Score

73. How does the program work?
<--- Score

74. Why is it important to register your apprenticeship program?
<--- Score

75. Are loyalty programs captured under regulations for financial services and financial products?
<--- Score

76. What are the fastest-growing parts of your business?
<--- Score

77. What incentives to the customers are created by the loyalty program in efforts to make them return?
<--- Score

78. Are you currently enrolled in a customer loyalty program?
<--- Score

79. Who should receive rewards?
<--- Score

80. Do the youth enjoy the program?
<--- Score

81. What if you hold elite status with one program?
<--- Score

82. What makes the best loyalty programs work?
<--- Score

83. How do you encourage your customers to visit quiet, backwater areas?
<--- Score

84. What makes for a good loyalty program - one that can actually help your organization improve the loyalty of its customers?
<--- Score

85. How does your organization utilize loyalty programs to increase market shares?
<--- Score

86. What is your satisfaction level with the overall quality of this enterprises goods (services)?
<--- Score

87. Have you already spoken to potential customers?
<--- Score

88. Do you purchase personal/vacation Amtrak tickets using your organization rate?
<--- Score

89. Are you ready to invest in promoting and marketing your loyalty program?
<--- Score

90. How does your organization incorporate

loyalty programs as part of its strategic business scheme?

<--- Score

91. What benefits can customers gain from being part of the loyalty program?

<--- Score

92. How would you describe a loyal customer in your own words?

<--- Score

93. What will be your contact strategy for your program members?

<--- Score

94. What constitutes a relationship?

<--- Score

95. What value care customers looking for in a hotel loyalty program?

<--- Score

96. How can a travel executive tell when one has come across a loyal customer?

<--- Score

97. Does your loyalty program have tiers?

<--- Score

98. Is your business turnover exploding through word of mouth?

<--- Score

99. What is your relationship with your manufacturers in your loyalty program?

<--- Score

100. How do you enroll in the Loyalty Program?
<--- Score

101. What role can a brand loyalty program play in a marketing strategy?
<--- Score

102. How do you reward your best customers and keep them engaged?
<--- Score

103. Are the benefits adequate?
<--- Score

104. What role does a digital presence play in the exhibition industry today, and why is it so important to get it right?
<--- Score

105. Is a loyalty program right for your business?
<--- Score

106. Are the vision, mission, goals, and objectives for the program intelligible and in writing?
<--- Score

107. Is there enough business to support everybody?
<--- Score

108. When should you use lifetime value?
<--- Score

109. Who attains social status?

<--- Score

110. What better way to see how well your loyalty program is working than by comparing your club members to the rest of your customer base?
<--- Score

111. How did the public react to the Loyalty Program?
<--- Score

112. Is it simple for customers to do business with you?
<--- Score

113. Is the program prominent on the website?
<--- Score

114. What if your referral orders a bundle of services?
<--- Score

115. How effective is your loyalty program?
<--- Score

116. How do you feel when you think of a certain brand?
<--- Score

117. How do you get the address of the current customer?
<--- Score

118. Are the key locations in the store supporting the correct product?
<--- Score

119. What qualities and capabilities should you look for in a gift and rewards partner?
<--- Score

120. How do you get information about your loyalty programs?
<--- Score

121. What is the skill level of your employees?
<--- Score

122. On what should the points be based?
<--- Score

123. Does your clients use loyalty card at any of your locations?
<--- Score

124. What do you like about the customer loyalty program(s) you are enrolled in?
<--- Score

125. Do you transfer your sales history to the corporate office?
<--- Score

126. Are your customers willing to go out of way to choose your products and services and refer them to others?
<--- Score

127. Is this support of the community and the arts public relations or an act of social responsibility?
<--- Score

128. Do you ever have a chance to tell you what you are personally interested in?
<--- Score

129. Are access features a hallmark?
<--- Score

130. Do you belong to loyalty programs at any of the already stated clubs?
<--- Score

131. What are customers willing to spend money on?
<--- Score

132. Does your organization have a position that touches in some way on the topic of corporate advertising and marketing in organizations?
<--- Score

133. Loyalty programs, shackle or reward: and to whom?
<--- Score

134. How close should you get to a customer when serving on the shop floor?
<--- Score

135. Who will do the artwork?
<--- Score

136. Do employees who use one service tend to use other services?
<--- Score

137. How do your members benefit from your

loyalty program?
<--- Score

138. What happens to your organizations current Loyalty Points?
<--- Score

139. What customer information should you track?
<--- Score

140. How smart is your loyalty program?
<--- Score

141. How will customers enroll?
<--- Score

142. What do you know about mobile applications for diabetes self-management?
<--- Score

143. How many legitimate organization or financial services pages reside on the same social media platform?
<--- Score

144. Are your loyal customers close to redeeming rewards?
<--- Score

145. How are your products selling across various customer behaviors?
<--- Score

146. What % of it clients drop out before reaching maintenance?
<--- Score

147. Does the shop display attract to the customers for purchase in convenience stores?
<--- Score

148. Which customers decreased spending and why?
<--- Score

149. When is the implementation of a personal Balanced Scorecard completed?
<--- Score

150. How did you (or your predecessor) start the loyalty program?
<--- Score

151. What are loyalty rewards programs?
<--- Score

152. How do you redeem your Loyalty Points?
<--- Score

153. Who is going to implement your social media strategy within your organization?
<--- Score

154. Why are loyalty or rewards program members so important?
<--- Score

155. What was the deciding factor when choosing the store from which you bought your suit?
<--- Score

156. What are team member responsibilities?

<--- Score

157. How will customers redeem benefits?
<--- Score

158. What is your reward tier level for your preferred hotel brands reward program?
<--- Score

159. Are you earning enough points to make your loyalty programs pay off?
<--- Score

160. What does your program stand for?
<--- Score

161. What makes customers come back?
<--- Score

162. How much domain knowledge is there in the team?
<--- Score

163. Are your team creating loyal customers, or just serving people?
<--- Score

164. How long has your loyalty program been in existence?
<--- Score

165. What makes loyalty programs fail?
<--- Score

166. What sort of guests should you look to enroll in your loyalty program?

<--- Score

167. What areas of your business operation provide the most frequent complaints?
<--- Score

168. What are the benefits of being a Key Member?
<--- Score

169. Why do customer attitudes towards loyalty programs matter a lot?
<--- Score

170. What types of program features and benefits does your loyalty program offer?
<--- Score

171. How often does the customer purchase?
<--- Score

172. Is interaction between the customers encouraged?
<--- Score

173. How likely is the customer likely to recommend your organization or the service?
<--- Score

174. How long does the average visitor stay in your community?
<--- Score

175. Are your satisfied customers loyal?
<--- Score

176. What image do you want to create of your

potential customer?

<--- Score

177. What is the scope (or market) of your program?

<--- Score

178. When you are the only business of your type in your area with this loyalty program, why would your customers go elsewhere?

<--- Score

179. How are you tracking your sales and inventory?

<--- Score

180. What is the population of your community?

<--- Score

181. What is your Rewards Currency?

<--- Score

182. How large is your current loyalty program?

<--- Score

183. What are the most profitable parts of your business?

<--- Score

184. What is your opinion about the loyalty card rules?

<--- Score

185. How does a customer feel about the already stated interactions?

<--- Score

186. Do you have to register in order to participate?
<--- Score

187. Which perceived benefits of a loyalty program will lead to more loyalty to your organization?
<--- Score

188. Is the customer willing to self-exclude?
<--- Score

189. What do you tell other shop owners who have been trying to find ways to boost business?
<--- Score

190. How will you know if you have changed levels?
<--- Score

191. Do the offerings in the online loyalty program have any expiration dates?
<--- Score

192. How do you know if a customer is a passionate fan a promoter?
<--- Score

193. What are factors that can contribute to a successful (effective) loyalty program?
<--- Score

194. How do successful loyalty programs differentiate themselves?
<--- Score

195. When is the last time you were asked for your e-mail address to join a loyalty program and, despite some curiosity and the possibility of a future discount, turned it down?
<--- Score

196. Are you collecting intel on your customers?
<--- Score

197. What industry-level initiatives are there?
<--- Score

198. How much do you value the rewards you receive from your loyalty program?
<--- Score

199. What if you only belong to one program?
<--- Score

200. Which elements determine a programs value from a customers perspective?
<--- Score

201. Do you use the information you store using one of your cloud services?
<--- Score

202. Does this look like a vacation you would want to take?
<--- Score

203. How do you determine success of your loyalty program?
<--- Score

204. Are other organizations in your community

using social media?
<--- Score

205. Do you have the right product in this area?
<--- Score

206. What should you do if you are a member of both programs?
<--- Score

207. Who joins a loyalty program?
<--- Score

208. Do reward programs truly build loyalty for lodging industry?
<--- Score

209. Do loyalty programs matter?
<--- Score

210. How does the internet influence price dispersion?
<--- Score

211. Does your customer loyalty program gain advantage for you?
<--- Score

212. Is there a product comparison option available within the online loyalty program?
<--- Score

213. How can a customer loyalty program create customer loyalty?
<--- Score

214. What aspects of your marketing efforts do you rely on a provider/vendor for?
<--- Score

215. What is a point worth?
<--- Score

216. Is the race track easy for the customer to follow, is it uncluttered, clean and safe?
<--- Score

217. How many people start hotel search on the mobile website or App and then move to the desktop?
<--- Score

218. How do you typically purchase print-related products and services for your business?
<--- Score

219. What value are customers looking for in a hotel loyalty program?
<--- Score

220. How do you choose a Cloud Service Provider and what are criteria to assess the choice?
<--- Score

221. What if a great percentage of the longer-term customers were already loyal?
<--- Score

222. Are you a transportation or service hub for surrounding communities?
<--- Score

223. Are certain customers more prone to participate in loyalty programs?

<--- Score

224. What are the objectives of this program?

<--- Score

225. How do you communicate your service strategy to your customers?

<--- Score

226. What are the effective dates of this program?

<--- Score

227. What is the degree of personalization or customization offered by loyalty programs?

<--- Score

228. What unique quality or feature of your community does it celebrate?

<--- Score

229. How did employees perceive the campaign and role in implementing it?

<--- Score

230. Are the reports received by the board and management appropriate and timely?

<--- Score

231. How should your organization frame program value toward customers long-term commitments?

<--- Score

232. What influences the relationship between customer satisfaction and repurchase intention?

<--- Score

233. How can a brand be used to target a specific market segment?
<--- Score

234. Which members left the program?
<--- Score

235. Why use rewards programs?
<--- Score

236. What are you expecting from a good loyalty program?
<--- Score

237. Are you regular customer of any convenience stores?
<--- Score

238. What are the effects of reward programs?
<--- Score

239. Should you invest in a loyalty program?
<--- Score

240. Describe the core, highest margin customer?
<--- Score

241. How many products should be bought?
<--- Score

242. What is the estimated number of clients on Immunotherapy in your practice?
<--- Score

243. Does your current customer loyalty program different from the old one?

<--- Score

244. Are products shown at all angles?

<--- Score

245. What should your technology spend be as a percentage of sales?

<--- Score

246. Which kind of relationship and how much relationship do which kind of service customers like?

<--- Score

247. Which partners should the program keep?

<--- Score

248. What kinds of rewards are preferred by your customers?

<--- Score

249. What distinguishes your program from other loyalty programs?

<--- Score

250. How can a retailer create a positive relationship with a manufacturer in customer loyalty program?

<--- Score

251. What do people want in a loyalty program?

<--- Score

252. What was the role of existing literature in the

start-up of the program?
<--- Score

253. (Is this/are) the best phone number/s to reach you on?
<--- Score

254. What are the most effective marketing channels in acquiring customers?
<--- Score

255. Are the water taxis glass enclosed?
<--- Score

256. Are you a member of a customer loyalty program within the beauty industry?
<--- Score

257. What were the reasons to implement the loyalty program?
<--- Score

258. Do vendors benefit from promotions in a multi-vendor loyalty program?
<--- Score

259. What is driving your customers to your store?
<--- Score

260. How does being a part of a loyalty program feel to you?
<--- Score

261. Does membership increase spend: verdict pending?
<--- Score

262. Which customers are the loyalty program targeting?
<--- Score

263. What is the business challenge?
<--- Score

264. Are the offerings in the loyalty program updated or changed?
<--- Score

265. How many and which companies use loyalty programs?
<--- Score

266. Where do you find more information about the program updates?
<--- Score

267. Is the airline and program leadership enabling the program to be successful?
<--- Score

268. What does this change mean to Loyalty Program Customers?
<--- Score

269. How will applications be reviewed?
<--- Score

270. Is the payment and payment security of the order handled by an external party?
<--- Score

271. How do you gain insights to direct supply-

chain activities and inventory placement across channels?

<--- Score

272. What are the pricing tactics in loyalty programs?

<--- Score

273. Why do many programs fail?

<--- Score

274. How/what will you receive notification that your friend/family members order has been confirmed and that you may redeem your reward?

<--- Score

275. What are procedures for the termination of cooperation in dispute?

<--- Score

276. How well do you monitor and manage your customers specific service/product purchase potential?

<--- Score

277. What types of mobile applications help associates be more efficient?

<--- Score

278. Are the familiar brands that customers ask for in the correct locations around the store?

<--- Score

279. How to sign an annual contract with a retail chain for production of store brand products?

<--- Score

280. Do loyalty programs matter at all in driving core customer restaurant brand loyalty?

<--- Score

281. Do you feel a personal connection to the brands that you hold a loyalty program membership with?

<--- Score

282. Are loyal customers profitable?

<--- Score

283. What should you do if a customer asks about being excluded?

<--- Score

284. Will you have to pay taxes on the amount of your Rewards?

<--- Score

285. What product and service categories are most adaptable to the fortitude and village concepts?

<--- Score

286. Where are your rewards?

<--- Score

287. Which customers?

<--- Score

288. Are your customers interested in greener companies or your corporate clients looking to green supply chain?

<--- Score

289. Do you want to accept gift certificates?
<--- Score

290. What are your business objectives?
<--- Score

291. What types of reports / incidents are available to customers?
<--- Score

292. Do you accrue points with your loyalty program which you can then turn in for rewards?
<--- Score

293. What is your best advice to companies that want to transform customer engagements?
<--- Score

294. Do you refer your business customers for residential service?
<--- Score

295. How are loyalty programs being applied effectively in practice and what are the key aspects?
<--- Score

296. How is your loyalty program performing?
<--- Score

297. Do customer loyalty programs really work?
<--- Score

298. How are consumers responding to your loyalty program?
<--- Score

299. Are you ever asked to account for loyalty programs to older family members?

<--- Score

300. Which businesses dominate your business category?

<--- Score

301. Why are you making changes to the Loyalty Program?

<--- Score

302. Which types of rewards do you get through your loyalty program?

<--- Score

303. How do you keep your business out of that one-third segment?

<--- Score

304. How might you expect a loyalty program to affect purchase loyalty indicators ?

<--- Score

305. Is the customer a consistent brand advocate?

<--- Score

306. Are you ready to involve partners in your loyalty program?

<--- Score

307. Why would someone who infrequently books a hotel go out of way to sign up for the Loyalty Program?

<--- Score

308. What is service design and why is it important for tourism?

<--- Score

309. Are you a chain store shopper or boutique enthusiast?

<--- Score

310. How many dedicated (full-time) employees support your loyalty program?

<--- Score

311. What is your competition offering its customers?

<--- Score

312. Do loyalty programs utilize new digital channels to reach customers?

<--- Score

313. Why do customers switch?

<--- Score

314. What is it worth to capture the already stated marginal customers with an extraordinary appeal?

<--- Score

315. How do customers react to different timing for rewards?

<--- Score

316. What factors motivate the adoption of clouds?

<--- Score

317. Have products reached them in a timely manner?

<--- Score

318. Could you claim that being part of a loyalty program leads a perception of good value among customers?

<--- Score

319. Which loyalty channels do guests prefer?

<--- Score

320. How many types of media does your organization use for a typical customer communication/marketing campaign?

<--- Score

321. Are your products or services complex?

<--- Score

322. What is the current status of customer loyalty program?

<--- Score

323. Do you think that customer loyalty programs are a good method to create loyalty among customers?

<--- Score

324. What are the target groups for the program?

<--- Score

325. How long have the loyalty program been active online?

<--- Score

326. Did you reach your current customers?
<--- Score

327. How much more do engaged members shop?
<--- Score

328. What are your organizations/organizations top reasons for blending print and digital media?
<--- Score

329. Which loyalty program influence to the customers for purchasing in convenience stores?
<--- Score

330. Does this mean you should stop marketing to gain new customers?
<--- Score

331. Will the program and its benefits change?
<--- Score

332. How does your program perform on a perceived funding rate basis?
<--- Score

333. What is your assessment of the user-friendliness of the customer loyalty program?
<--- Score

334. What is your opinion about the membership price?
<--- Score

335. How are you promoting your Program?
<--- Score

336. Loyalty programs, shackle or reward?
<--- Score

337. What is your brands mobile strategy?
<--- Score

338. How to gain loyalty in the first place?
<--- Score

339. Building loyalty by encouraging disloyalty?
<--- Score

340. Which customer segment has a potential to increase your revenue?
<--- Score

341. What kind of relational benefits provide programs?
<--- Score

342. Do you sell directly to your customers?
<--- Score

343. What are the measurable marketing objectives of your program?
<--- Score

344. What are some social media trends?
<--- Score

345. How does all of this affect the program participant?
<--- Score

346. Why use tools of service design in context of a customer loyalty program?

<--- Score

347. What is the most important factor when choosing the store for a suit purchase?
<--- Score

348. Where do you find more details about this program?
<--- Score

349. What would you like to do at the end of your lease?
<--- Score

350. Does visualization encourage customers to engage more with the program?
<--- Score

351. What changes have been made to Loyalty Program recently?
<--- Score

352. What makes the soft brand concept so revolutionary?
<--- Score

353. What is the right number of members to have in your program?
<--- Score

354. Do you run a loyalty program and a gift card program for the same store?
<--- Score

355. What is the value, the function, the purpose?
<--- Score

356. Are customers satisfied with your current loyalty program?
<--- Score

357. What prevents them from joining a loyalty program?
<--- Score

358. Does a customer loyalty program actually create loyalty?
<--- Score

359. Is your store front clean and inviting to the customer?
<--- Score

360. Do your manufacturers also doing own brand loyalty program to the customers?
<--- Score

361. How many consumers approximately participate in the loyalty program?
<--- Score

362. Why are loyalty programs worth it?
<--- Score

363. Do loyalty programs really work, or are companies just wasting money?
<--- Score

364. How easy is it to contact your organization?
<--- Score

365. Have you collected any feedback from your

community and additional stakeholders about your work?

<--- Score

366. Does your electric utility have active employee or community engagement programs?

<--- Score

367. Who is the program for?

<--- Score

368. Which rewards are most attractive?

<--- Score

369. How is your program unique?

<--- Score

370. How can frequent shopper programs be successful in the grocery industry?

<--- Score

371. Do reward programs, also called loyalty programs, work?

<--- Score

372. How many steps is it to get in the rewards program?

<--- Score

373. Do you think that membership cards create loyalty among the customers?

<--- Score

374. Is the card for loyalty rewards only or for other functions, as stored value?

<--- Score

375. Do you commit to social media success?
<--- Score

376. How the previous experience has been for the customer ?
<--- Score

377. What is the logo, mascot, or brand mark?
<--- Score

378. How do people benefit from the loyalty program?
<--- Score

379. Does this function to just give free rewards to your existing customers?
<--- Score

380. How long will you maintain your level?
<--- Score

381. What is customer satisfaction and what is loyalty?
<--- Score

382. When determining target audience, businesses often consider questions: Who will see the most value in your products or services?
<--- Score

383. Is there an effort underway to partner with a product delivery service?
<--- Score

384. What kind of vacation would appeal to people

in this niche?

<--- Score

385. Do you separate all your locations so that your clients can only use local brunch?

<--- Score

386. What do the top 15 percent know that other sales people don t?

<--- Score

387. What are the benefits and limitations of using social media?

<--- Score

388. What is the future of loyalty?

<--- Score

389. Is this the right way to approach employee loyalty?

<--- Score

390. How ideal is the product (service)?

<--- Score

391. What are the benefits of joining multiple programs versus joining a select few?

<--- Score

392. How do you achieve top tier status?

<--- Score

393. What is/are the objective(s) of your program?

<--- Score

394. How does prior experience(s) with reward

programs influence loyalty, commitment, and reward accumulating behavior?

<--- Score

395. Revenue management and customer centric marketing - how do they influence travellers choices?

<--- Score

396. Who are your most valuable customers?

<--- Score

397. How do you end your program one day?

<--- Score

398. What are social media outreach tactics?

<--- Score

399. Do you have a single view of a customers participation?

<--- Score

400. How does a customers activity compare before joining the program versus after joining the program?

<--- Score

401. What percentage of your customer base is enrolled in your customer loyalty program?

<--- Score

402. What program attributes are most important to customers?

<--- Score

403. What are the Tier Levels?

<--- Score

404. How would the interviewee describe your organizations loyalty program?
<--- Score

405. How do you assess how well the common reading program works?
<--- Score

406. Which segment would be the one core customer?
<--- Score

407. Do you provide information for phone books and Caller ID?
<--- Score

408. Is the brand name product substantially different from the generic?
<--- Score

409. How do you become eligible for membership benefits?
<--- Score

410. How does a web page retrieve and display the email address of a customer?
<--- Score

411. How has social media changed the concept of loyalty marketing?
<--- Score

412. Do loyalty program membership and status levels affect service customers choices?

<--- Score

413. How can it be used as part of a marketing strategy?
<--- Score

414. Does the payment relate to a specific promised good or service that transfers to the customer?
<--- Score

415. What should loyal customers honestly receive from organization of choice?
<--- Score

416. Does the community want to permit/ encourage/explore alternative energy sources?
<--- Score

417. Who are your Program Ambassadors?
<--- Score

418. How do loyalty programs boost retention?
<--- Score

419. What is your favorite loyalty program?
<--- Score

420. How will customers be rewarded?
<--- Score

421. How will the program be structured?
<--- Score

422. What is the legacy of the Employee Loyalty Program?

<--- Score

423. Does sales information exist for each of your products?
<--- Score

424. Which customers are at your shop right now?
<--- Score

425. What do guests want from a restaurant loyalty program?
<--- Score

426. What is favorite restaurant loyalty program?
<--- Score

427. What kind of incentives would you like to see from this program?
<--- Score

428. What are the benefits of loyalty programs using credit debit cards?
<--- Score

429. What type of program and structure?
<--- Score

430. How do you incentivize occasional customers to become regular or weekly customers?
<--- Score

431. Should you delight the customer?
<--- Score

432. What is the value of loyalty bonus programs?
<--- Score

433. Does the loyalty program help you gamble more responsibly?

<--- Score

434. Are staff able to direct customers to resources?

<--- Score

435. What countries are participating in the Loyalty Program?

<--- Score

436. What are the changes in sales frequency and/ or volume due to the program?

<--- Score

437. Does the store have a designated sections for wellness products?

<--- Score

438. Do enhancements to loyalty programs affect demand?

<--- Score

439. What potential customers already exist in your region and/or community?

<--- Score

440. Which capabilities/components does your customer loyalty program use?

<--- Score

441. What is your opinion about your manufacturers brand loyalty program?

<--- Score

442. Does the program generate new consumers?
<--- Score

443. How can blockchain tokenization help build a robust loyalty program?
<--- Score

444. Can the name/logo be used in all desirable applications?
<--- Score

445. What does the phrase customer loyalty mean to you?
<--- Score

446. Do you encourage older family members to join loyalty programs?
<--- Score

447. Do loyalty programs increase spending?
<--- Score

448. Will sales be better or worse?
<--- Score

449. What are the price differences between wellness and traditional products?
<--- Score

450. Will the friends relationship remain the same?
<--- Score

451. When do you consider outsourcing the member database, the loyalty program web site, and other facets of the loyalty program?

<--- Score

452. When should stock levels increase?
<--- Score

453. Do you have a bar tenders guide pull up in order mode?
<--- Score

454. Is your recruiting, training and promotions oriented towards customer service?
<--- Score

455. Will customers make enough purchases to receive benefits from the program?
<--- Score

456. Do linear loyalty programs provide a competitive advantage?
<--- Score

457. How much do you value your employees?
<--- Score

458. Why do you think companies have loyalty programs?
<--- Score

459. How long have you been a member of this loyalty program?
<--- Score

460. If you did not get the business, who would?
<--- Score

461. Is inactivity in the online loyalty program

penalized?

<--- Score

462. Do you send out marketing communications to your loyalty customers?

<--- Score

463. Do satisfied clients depend on satisfied employees?

<--- Score

464. What type of benefits do they desire the most?

<--- Score

465. What do you use your loyalty benefits toward?

<--- Score

466. Is your small business too small to implement a customer loyalty program?

<--- Score

467. What is it going to cost to build, maintain, and refine your customer loyalty program on an ongoing basis?

<--- Score

468. How long are Loyalty Points valid?

<--- Score

469. What classes, majors, or programs does your organization offer that appeal to you?

<--- Score

470. Are frequent-guest programs effective?

<--- Score

471. Have the goals set on the loyalty program changed from its inception?
<--- Score

472. When you begin to launch the customer loyalty program to your customers?
<--- Score

473. What is the influence of loyalty programs on purchase intention?
<--- Score

474. Are you a member of your preferred hotel brands reward program?
<--- Score

475. What could be so hard about a simple loyalty program?
<--- Score

476. Which type of program suits your business?
<--- Score

477. Does the loyalty program have a specific name?
<--- Score

478. How to capture a greater percentage of market share while keeping customers loyal to the brand?
<--- Score

479. Why might this project not work?
<--- Score

480. What are the promised goods or services in a contract with a customer?

<--- Score

481. Is it a short incentive program or long-term loyalty program?

<--- Score

482. What do you attribute that to higher passenger satisfaction?

<--- Score

483. Does this mean the loyalty empire is rotting from within?

<--- Score

484. Regarding your loyalty programs: How valuable is valuable enough?

<--- Score

485. What is your assessment of the range of offers of the customer loyalty program?

<--- Score

486. Can preferred customers participate in the loyalty program?

<--- Score

487. How might you attract that niche to your community?

<--- Score

488. Do economic rewards work?

<--- Score

489. What is the ease of access for the customer to interact with your organization or the service?

<--- Score

490. Does your customer loyalty program increase customers favor of your brand?

<--- Score

491. How is the loyalty program promoted among your customers?

<--- Score

492. What is the rate of annual turnover of sales representatives?

<--- Score

493. What do you expect from the Cloud?

<--- Score

494. What is the hardest part about your job?

<--- Score

495. How should your organization protect customer information?

<--- Score

496. How does your organization make full use of customer information?

<--- Score

497. How appealing are each retailer loyalty features to you?

<--- Score

498. What professional relationships have you established?

<--- Score

499. What has digital marketing done to loyalty marketing and how should companies utilize it?
<--- Score

500. How will this program fit with the brand vision?
<--- Score

501. What do your employees know in order to deliver the best customer service?
<--- Score

502. What should a brand do if it has low awareness and a positive image?
<--- Score

503. What are the rewards or benefits that consumers in Taiwan value the most?
<--- Score

504. What are the greatest challenges facing your customer loyalty initiatives today?
<--- Score

505. How complex and embedded within an enterprise are the products and services that you sell?
<--- Score

506. What are the core objectives of the program?
<--- Score

507. How does your loyalty program serve the overarching goals of the business?

<--- Score

508. Do loyalty programs really enhance behavioral loyalty?
<--- Score

509. When thinking of what to offer your customers ask yourself - If you read this, would the offer be good enough to make you respond?
<--- Score

510. How should your organization address service failures in loyalty programs?
<--- Score

511. How should your organization differentiate the brands and cope with market competition via loyalty programs?
<--- Score

512. What are the determining characteristics, more generally, of returns to loyalty?
<--- Score

513. How long should a customer be kept in a service loaner?
<--- Score

514. How much less do disappointed members shop?
<--- Score

515. What do you like to see in a brand mark?
<--- Score

516. Will the program be points-based or have a

tiered reward structure?

<--- Score

517. How fast do you get to the elite status?

<--- Score

518. Can family members link or share an account?

<--- Score

519. Will it be everyone or just the business best customers?

<--- Score

520. Do you afford to launch your own digital customer loyalty program?

<--- Score

521. Does your product & service portfolio fit with your customers?

<--- Score

522. What kinds of social media are you trying?

<--- Score

523. How is loyalty created within the customer loyalty program?

<--- Score

524. How will this all look to the customer?

<--- Score

525. Do you match status with other loyalty programs?

<--- Score

526. What value proposition are you offering?

<--- Score

527. Does your store reflect a personality to your customers?
<--- Score

528. Has your loyalty program been getting away from you?
<--- Score

529. What happens if you edit or cancel an order, and create a new one in the same month?
<--- Score

530. What sort of program should you use to reach your objectives?
<--- Score

531. Are you currently an active member of a sporting, hobby or community-based club or association?
<--- Score

532. How will customers earn rewards?
<--- Score

533. How does your organization establish customer commitment toward loyalty programs?
<--- Score

534. Why do you want a program?
<--- Score

535. How effective are rewards programs in achieving behavioral loyalty?
<--- Score

536. What have been the recent trends in the loyalty industry?
<--- Score

537. What sorts of social media channels do you use to communicate with your customer base?
<--- Score

538. Is the nature of your business relationship transactional?
<--- Score

539. What perks are most appealing to new members who sign up for the Loyalty Program?
<--- Score

540. Do loyalty programs really enhance behavioural loyalty?
<--- Score

541. How do you create a compelling loyalty program that will take members or employees by surprise, create meaningful connections, and reinforce value to your organization?
<--- Score

542. Do loyalty programs have the actual effectiveness to create loyalty?
<--- Score

543. What are the rewards?
<--- Score

544. Do you know what kind and how much waste your business generates?

<--- Score

545. Are loyalty programs best managed in-house or contracted out?
<--- Score

546. How satisfied are you with the customer loyalty program?
<--- Score

547. How do you stop guests from leaving your program?
<--- Score

548. Have you thought of running a loyalty program for your online store?
<--- Score

549. How do you begin offering that type of fast, accurate and personalized service?
<--- Score

550. What is the primary tool used by a sales-oriented organization to achieve its corporate goals?
<--- Score

551. Do you think a customer loyalty program is necessary?
<--- Score

552. Are your programs rewards, tiers and benefits aligned to member value?
<--- Score

553. What is the future of customer engagement?

<--- Score

554. Brand loyalty - what where how much?
<--- Score

555. When is consumer activity with loyalty programs the highest, beginning, middle or end?
<--- Score

556. Do you refer business customers?
<--- Score

557. Is loyalty attainable?
<--- Score

558. What can a loyalty program do for your business?
<--- Score

559. Does your loyalty program have Yes tiers?
<--- Score

560. What do you offer your customers?
<--- Score

561. How will you communicate with customers?
<--- Score

Add up total points for this section:
_ _ _ _ _ = Total points for this section

Divided by: _ _ _ _ _ _ (number of statements answered) = _ _ _ _ _ _
Average score for this section

Transfer your score to the Loyalty

Program Index at the beginning of the
Self-Assessment.

Loyalty Program and Managing Projects, Criteria for Project Managers:

1.0 Initiating Process Group: Loyalty Program

1. Measurable - are the targets measurable?

2. How will you know you did it?

3. What do they need to know about the Loyalty Program project?

4. Do you know if the Loyalty Program project requires outside equipment or vendor resources?

5. When must it be done?

6. What are the inputs required to produce the deliverables?

7. In which Loyalty Program project management process group is the detailed Loyalty Program project budget created?

8. Mitigate. what will you do to minimize the impact should the risk event occur?

9. Although the Loyalty Program project manager does not directly manage procurement and contracting activities, who does manage procurement and contracting activities in your organization then if not the PM?

10. Information sharing?

11. First of all, should any action be taken?

12. Realistic - are the desired results expressed in a way that the team will be motivated and believe that the required level of involvement will be obtained?

13. Contingency planning. if a risk event occurs, what will you do?

14. Do you understand the quality and control criteria that must be achieved for successful Loyalty Program project completion?

15. What will you do?

16. If action is called for, what form should it take?

17. What are the constraints?

18. The process to Manage Stakeholders is part of which process group?

19. Where must it be done?

20. What communication items need improvement?

1.1 Project Charter: Loyalty Program

21. Run it as as a startup?

22. Why do you manage integration?

23. What ideas do you have for initial tests of change (PDSA cycles)?

24. Why is it important?

25. Whose input and support will this Loyalty Program project require?

26. How will you know that a change is an improvement?

27. What is the purpose of the Loyalty Program project?

28. What are the assigned resources?

29. Is it an improvement over existing products?

30. If finished, on what date did it finish?

31. What metrics could you look at?

32. Are there special technology requirements?

33. Loyalty Program project background: what is the primary motivation for this Loyalty Program project?

34. What material?

35. How high should you set your goals?

36. Customer: who are you doing the Loyalty Program project for?

37. How much?

38. Why is a Loyalty Program project Charter used?

39. Strategic fit: what is the strategic initiative identifier for this Loyalty Program project?

40. When?

1.2 Stakeholder Register: Loyalty Program

41. How will reports be created?

42. How big is the gap?

43. What is the power of the stakeholder?

44. Who are the stakeholders?

45. How should employers make voices heard?

46. How much influence do they have on the Loyalty Program project?

47. Is your organization ready for change?

48. Who wants to talk about Security?

49. What opportunities exist to provide communications?

50. Who is managing stakeholder engagement?

51. What are the major Loyalty Program project milestones requiring communications or providing communications opportunities?

52. What & Why?

1.3 Stakeholder Analysis Matrix: Loyalty Program

53. Is there a clear description of the scope of practice of the Loyalty Program projects educators?

54. Environmental effects?

55. Who has not been involved up to now and should have been?

56. How to measure the achievement of the Development Objective?

57. How do customers express needs?

58. Who holds positions of responsibility in interested organizations?

59. Who will be affected by the Loyalty Program project?

60. How do you manage Loyalty Program project Risk?

61. Which conditions out of the control of the management are crucial to contribute for the achievement of the development objective?

62. Usps (unique selling points)?

63. Who is most dependent on the resources at stake?

64. What is your organizations competitors doing?

65. What are the key services, contractual arrangements, or other relationships between stakeholder groups?

66. What do you need to appraise?

67. New USPs?

68. What tools would help you communicate?

69. Why do you need to manage Loyalty Program project Risk?

70. Accreditations, etc?

71. Who will be affected by the work?

72. Would it be fair to say that cost is a controlling criteria?

2.0 Planning Process Group: Loyalty Program

73. Did the program design/ implementation strategy adequately address the planning stage necessary to set up structures, hire staff etc.?

74. How does activity resource estimation affect activity duration estimation?

75. Will the products created live up to the necessary quality?

76. Does the program have follow-up mechanisms (to verify the quality of the products, punctuality of delivery, etc.) to measure progress in the achievement of the envisaged results?

77. To what extent have public/private national resources and/or counterparts been mobilized to contribute to the programs objective and produce results and impacts?

78. How are it Loyalty Program projects different?

79. What is the critical path for this Loyalty Program project, and what is the duration of the critical path?

80. Are the follow-up indicators relevant and do they meet the quality needed to measure the outputs and outcomes of the Loyalty Program project?

81. In what way has the Loyalty Program project come

up with innovative measures for problem-solving?

82. How will users learn how to use the deliverables?

83. What factors are contributing to progress or delay in the achievement of products and results?

84. What is the NEXT thing to do?

85. What will you do to minimize the impact should a risk event occur?

86. How well did the chosen processes fit the needs of the Loyalty Program project?

87. Why is it important to determine activity sequencing on Loyalty Program projects?

88. What should you do next?

89. What are the different approaches to building the WBS?

90. Have more efficient (sensitive) and appropriate measures been adopted to respond to the political and socio-cultural problems identified?

91. Professionals want to know what is expected from them; what are the deliverables?

2.1 Project Management Plan: Loyalty Program

92. What goes into your Loyalty Program project Charter?

93. Has the selected plan been formulated using cost effectiveness and incremental analysis techniques?

94. Are there any client staffing expectations?

95. What are the known stakeholder requirements?

96. When is the Loyalty Program project management plan created?

97. Are there any windfall benefits that would accrue to the Loyalty Program project sponsor or other parties?

98. How do you manage time?

99. How can you best help your organization to develop consistent practices in Loyalty Program project management planning stages?

100. What data/reports/tools/etc. do program managers need?

101. What are the deliverables?

102. Development trends and opportunities. What if the positive direction and vision of your organization

causes expected trends to change?

103. What went right?

104. How do you organize the costs in the Loyalty Program project management plan?

105. Does the implementation plan have an appropriate division of responsibilities?

106. Are cost risk analysis methods applied to develop contingencies for the estimated total Loyalty Program project costs?

107. Are comparable cost estimates used for comparing, screening and selecting alternative plans, and has a reasonable cost estimate been developed for the recommended plan?

108. What is the business need?

109. Why Change?

110. Did the planning effort collaborate to develop solutions that integrate expertise, policies, programs, and Loyalty Program projects across entities?

2.2 Scope Management Plan: Loyalty Program

111. Have reserves been created to address risks?

112. Deliverables -are the deliverables tangible and verifiable?

113. Were Loyalty Program project team members involved in the development of activity & task decomposition?

114. Describe the process for accepting the Loyalty Program project deliverables. Will the Loyalty Program project deliverables become accepted in writing?

115. What is the estimated cost of creating and implementing?

116. Is quality monitored from the perspective of the customers needs and expectations?

117. Cost / benefit analysis?

118. What are the acceptance criteria (process and criteria to be met for key stakeholder acceptance) and who is authorized to sign off?

119. Is there any form of automated support for Issues Management?

120. Pop quiz – what changed on Loyalty Program project scope statement input?

121. Has the Loyalty Program project manager been identified?

122. What if you do not have more detailed information on the report?

123. Are all payments made according to the contract(s)?

124. Are Loyalty Program project team members involved in detailed estimating and scheduling?

125. How are you planning to maintain the scope baseline and how will you manage scope changes?

126. Sensitivity analysis?

127. What are the Quality Assurance overheads?

128. Are software metrics formally captured, analyzed and used as a basis for other Loyalty Program project estimates?

129. Has allowance been made for vacations, holidays, training (learning time for each team member), staff promotions & staff turnovers?

130. Has your organization done similar tasks before?

2.3 Requirements Management Plan: Loyalty Program

131. Do you understand the role that each stakeholder will play in the requirements process?

132. If it exists, where is it housed?

133. Could inaccurate or incomplete requirements in this Loyalty Program project create a serious risk for the business?

134. Do you have an agreed upon process for alerting the Loyalty Program project Manager if a request for change in requirements leads to a product scope change?

135. Which hardware or software, related to, or as outcome of the Loyalty Program project is new to your organization?

136. How detailed should the Loyalty Program project get?

137. How will you develop the schedule of requirements activities?

138. Who will perform the analysis?

139. The wbs is developed as part of a Joint planning session. and how do you know that youhave done this right?

140. Will the contractors involved take full responsibility?

141. Will you use an assessment of the Loyalty Program project environment as a tool to discover risk to the requirements process?

142. Will you use tracing to help understand the impact of a change in requirements?

143. Is infrastructure setup part of your Loyalty Program project?

144. Will the Loyalty Program project requirements become approved in writing?

145. Are all the stakeholders ready for the transition into the user community?

146. Should you include sub-activities?

147. Will the product release be stable and mature enough to be deployed in the user community?

148. Is any organizational data being used or stored?

149. Is there formal agreement on who has authority to approve a change in requirements?

150. Is there formal agreement on who has authority to request a change in requirements?

2.4 Requirements Documentation: Loyalty Program

151. What are the potential disadvantages/ advantages?

152. How linear / iterative is your Requirements Gathering process (or will it be)?

153. How much testing do you need to do to prove that your system is safe?

154. What can tools do for us?

155. Where do you define what is a customer, what are the attributes of customer?

156. What images does it conjure?

157. Are there legal issues?

158. What is your Elevator Speech?

159. Is new technology needed?

160. Completeness. are all functions required by the customer included?

161. Does the system provide the functions which best support the customers needs?

162. How will the proposed Loyalty Program project help?

163. Have the benefits identified with the system being identified clearly?

164. The problem with gathering requirements is right there in the word gathering. What images does it conjure?

165. Do technical resources exist?

166. Where do system and software requirements come from, what are sources?

167. Has requirements gathering uncovered information that would necessitate changes?

168. Basic work/business process; high-level, what is being touched?

169. What is a show stopper in the requirements?

170. What is effective documentation?

2.5 Requirements Traceability Matrix: Loyalty Program

171. What are the chronologies, contingencies, consequences, criteria?

172. Will you use a Requirements Traceability Matrix?

173. Why use a WBS?

174. How will it affect the stakeholders personally in career?

175. What is the WBS?

176. What percentage of Loyalty Program projects are producing traceability matrices between requirements and other work products?

177. Describe the process for approving requirements so they can be added to the traceability matrix and Loyalty Program project work can be performed. Will the Loyalty Program project requirements become approved in writing?

178. How do you manage scope?

179. Is there a requirements traceability process in place?

180. How small is small enough?

181. Why do you manage scope?

182. Do you have a clear understanding of all subcontracts in place?

2.6 Project Scope Statement: Loyalty Program

183. What are the possible consequences should a risk come to occur?

184. Is an issue management process documented and filed?

185. Is the Loyalty Program project organization documented and on file?

186. If there is an independent oversight contractor, have they signed off on the Loyalty Program project Plan?

187. Relevant - ask yourself can you get there; why are you doing this Loyalty Program project?

188. Has everyone approved the Loyalty Program projects scope statement?

189. Is there an information system for the Loyalty Program project?

190. How will you verify the accuracy of the work of the Loyalty Program project, and what constitutes acceptance of the deliverables?

191. Are there completion/verification criteria defined for each task producing an output?

192. Are there backup strategies for key members of

the Loyalty Program project?

193. Is the plan for your organization of the Loyalty Program project resources adequate?

194. What went wrong?

195. What should you drop in order to add something new?

196. If you were to write a list of what should not be included in the scope statement, what are the things that you would recommend be described as out-of-scope?

197. Have the reports to be produced, distributed, and filed been defined?

198. Will the risk status be reported to management on a regular and frequent basis?

199. Risks?

200. Who will you recommend approve the change, and when do you recommend the change reviews occur?

201. Elements that deal with providing the detail?

202. Is the change control process documented and on file?

2.7 Assumption and Constraint Log: Loyalty Program

203. What to do at recovery?

204. Are there standards for code development?

205. When can log be discarded?

206. Does the document/deliverable meet general requirements (for example, statement of work) for all deliverables?

207. Are there nonconformance issues?

208. Can you perform this task or activity in a more effective manner?

209. Have adequate resources been provided by management to ensure Loyalty Program project success?

210. No superfluous information or marketing narrative?

211. Does the traceability documentation describe the tool and/or mechanism to be used to capture traceability throughout the life cycle?

212. If it is out of compliance, should the process be amended or should the Plan be amended?

213. Is there adequate stakeholder participation for

the vetting of requirements definition, changes and management?

214. If appropriate, is the deliverable content consistent with current Loyalty Program project documents and in compliance with the Document Management Plan?

215. Are requirements management tracking tools and procedures in place?

216. Have you eliminated all duplicative tasks or manual efforts, where appropriate?

217. Has the approach and development strategy of the Loyalty Program project been defined, documented and accepted by the appropriate stakeholders?

218. Are processes for release management of new development from coding and unit testing, to integration testing, to training, and production defined and followed?

219. Have all involved stakeholders and work groups committed to the Loyalty Program project?

220. Contradictory information between document sections?

221. Violation trace: why ?

222. How are new requirements or changes to requirements identified?

2.8 Work Breakdown Structure: Loyalty Program

223. Why would you develop a Work Breakdown Structure?

224. Why is it useful?

225. Do you need another level?

226. How many levels?

227. Can you make it?

228. How big is a work-package?

229. When do you stop?

230. How will you and your Loyalty Program project team define the Loyalty Program projects scope and work breakdown structure?

231. Is it still viable?

232. What is the probability of completing the Loyalty Program project in less that xx days?

233. How far down?

234. When does it have to be done?

235. When would you develop a Work Breakdown Structure?

236. Is it a change in scope?

237. Where does it take place?

238. What is the probability that the Loyalty Program project duration will exceed xx weeks?

239. Is the work breakdown structure (wbs) defined and is the scope of the Loyalty Program project clear with assigned deliverable owners?

240. How much detail?

2.9 WBS Dictionary: Loyalty Program

241. Does the contractors system provide unit or lot costs when applicable?

242. Does the scheduling system identify in a timely manner the status of work?

243. Are meaningful indicators identified for use in measuring the status of cost and schedule performance?

244. Are records maintained to show how undistributed budgets are controlled?

245. The already stated responsible for overhead performance control of related costs?

246. The total budget for the contract (including estimates for authorized and unpriced work)?

247. Appropriate work authorization documents which subdivide the contractual effort and responsibilities, within functional organizations?

248. What size should a work package be?

249. Is each control account assigned to a single organizational element directly responsible for the work and identifiable to a single element of the CWBS?

250. Are there procedures for monitoring action items and corrective actions to the point of resolution and

are corresponding procedures being followed?

251. Is undistributed budget limited to contract effort which cannot yet be planned to CWBS elements at or below the level specified for reporting to the Government?

252. Is future work which cannot be planned in detail subdivided to the extent practicable for budgeting and scheduling purposes?

253. Are the overhead pools formally and adequately identified?

254. Changes in the overhead pool and/or organization structures?

255. Knowledgeable Loyalty Program projections of future performance?

256. What are you counting on?

257. Is subcontracted work defined and identified to the appropriate subcontractor within the proper WBS element?

258. Budgets assigned to control accounts?

259. Are your organizations and items of cost assigned to each pool identified?

260. Is work properly classified as measured effort, LOE, or apportioned effort and appropriately separated?

2.10 Schedule Management Plan: Loyalty Program

261. Have Loyalty Program project success criteria been defined?

262. Has a quality assurance plan been developed for the Loyalty Program project?

263. Is the plan consistent with industry best practices?

264. Is a process defined for baseline approval and control?

265. Are the quality tools and methods identified in the Quality Plan appropriate to the Loyalty Program project?

266. Is there an approved case?

267. What will be the format of the schedule model?

268. Is documentation created for communication with the suppliers and Vendors?

269. Goal: is the schedule feasible and at what cost?

270. Are assumptions being identified, recorded, analyzed, qualified and closed?

271. Are trade-offs between accepting the risk and mitigating the risk identified?

272. Is your organization certified as a broker of the products/supplies?

273. Have all team members been part of identifying risks?

274. Has a sponsor been identified?

275. What strengths do you have?

276. Have Loyalty Program project management standards and procedures been identified / established and documented?

277. Are all resource assumptions documented?

278. Are the processes for schedule assessment and analysis defined?

279. Is there an issues management plan in place?

2.11 Activity List: Loyalty Program

280. Is infrastructure setup part of your Loyalty Program project?

281. Where will it be performed?

282. How difficult will it be to do specific activities on this Loyalty Program project?

283. What did not go as well?

284. What will be performed?

285. What are the critical bottleneck activities?

286. How do you determine the late start (LS) for each activity?

287. What is the probability the Loyalty Program project can be completed in xx weeks?

288. How will it be performed?

289. For other activities, how much delay can be tolerated?

290. How should ongoing costs be monitored to try to keep the Loyalty Program project within budget?

291. What is your organizations history in doing similar activities?

292. How much slack is available in the Loyalty

Program project?

293. When will the work be performed?

294. What went well?

295. What is the total time required to complete the Loyalty Program project if no delays occur?

296. How can the Loyalty Program project be displayed graphically to better visualize the activities?

2.12 Activity Attributes: Loyalty Program

297. How difficult will it be to do specific activities on this Loyalty Program project?

298. Have you identified the Activity Leveling Priority code value on each activity?

299. Resource is assigned to?

300. What is missing?

301. Are the required resources available or need to be acquired?

302. Have constraints been applied to the start and finish milestones for the phases?

303. Activity: fair or not fair?

304. Resources to accomplish the work?

305. Can more resources be added?

306. How many resources do you need to complete the work scope within a limit of X number of days?

307. How else could the items be grouped?

308. How many days do you need to complete the work scope with a limit of X number of resources?

309. Does your organization of the data change its meaning?

310. Do you feel very comfortable with your prediction?

311. Why?

312. How much activity detail is required?

313. Is there a trend during the year?

314. Would you consider either of corresponding activities an outlier?

2.13 Milestone List: Loyalty Program

315. Calculate how long can activity be delayed?

316. How late can each activity be finished and started?

317. Legislative effects?

318. What background experience, skills, and strengths does the team bring to your organization?

319. Level of the Innovation?

320. Do you foresee any technical risks or developmental challenges?

321. What specific improvements did you make to the Loyalty Program project proposal since the previous time?

322. Vital contracts and partners?

323. How late can the activity finish?

324. How will the milestone be verified?

325. Marketing - reach, distribution, awareness?

326. How will you get the word out to customers?

327. What is the market for your technology, product or service?

328. What date will the task finish?

329. Sustaining internal capabilities?

330. Milestone pages should display the UserID of the person who added the milestone. Does a report or query exist that provides this audit information?

331. Describe your organizations strengths and core competencies. What factors will make your organization succeed?

332. Effects on core activities, distraction?

2.14 Network Diagram: Loyalty Program

333. Will crashing x weeks return more in benefits than it costs?

334. What are the tools?

335. What is the lowest cost to complete this Loyalty Program project in xx weeks?

336. What job or jobs could run concurrently?

337. What job or jobs follow it?

338. Review the logical flow of the network diagram. Take a look at which activities you have first and then sequence the activities. Do they make sense?

339. Exercise: what is the probability that the Loyalty Program project duration will exceed xx weeks?

340. Where do you schedule uncertainty time?

341. What can be done concurrently?

342. What are the Major Administrative Issues?

343. Why must you schedule milestones, such as reviews, throughout the Loyalty Program project?

344. What activities must follow this activity?

345. Can you calculate the confidence level?

346. Are you on time?

347. What are the Key Success Factors?

348. If the Loyalty Program project network diagram cannot change and you have extra personnel resources, what is the BEST thing to do?

349. What must be completed before an activity can be started?

350. What controls the start and finish of a job?

2.15 Activity Resource Requirements: Loyalty Program

351. What is the Work Plan Standard?

352. Anything else?

353. Organizational Applicability?

354. Time for overtime?

355. How many signatures do you require on a check and does this match what is in your policy and procedures?

356. What are constraints that you might find during the Human Resource Planning process?

357. Are there unresolved issues that need to be addressed?

358. How do you handle petty cash?

359. When does monitoring begin?

360. Other support in specific areas?

361. Do you use tools like decomposition and rolling-wave planning to produce the activity list and other outputs?

362. Is there anything planned that does not need to be here?

363. Which logical relationship does the PDM use most often?

364. Why do you do that?

2.16 Resource Breakdown Structure: Loyalty Program

365. What can you do to improve productivity?

366. Who is allowed to see what data about which resources?

367. What are the requirements for resource data?

368. Changes based on input from stakeholders?

369. What defines a successful Loyalty Program project?

370. The list could probably go on, but, the thing that you would most like to know is, How long & How much?

371. What is each stakeholders desired outcome for the Loyalty Program project?

372. What is the difference between % Complete and % work?

373. Goals for the Loyalty Program project. What is each stakeholders desired outcome for the Loyalty Program project?

374. What defines a successful Loyalty Program project?

375. Why do you do it?

376. Who will be used as a Loyalty Program project team member?

377. Are the required resources available?

378. Is predictive resource analysis being done?

379. Which resource planning tool provides information on resource responsibility and accountability?

2.17 Activity Duration Estimates: Loyalty Program

380. Which does one need in order to complete schedule development?

381. Will the new application negatively affect the current IT infrastructure?

382. What are the options you found to help people prepare for the exam?

383. What are some general rules of thumb for deciding if cost variance, schedule variance, cost performance index, and schedule performance index numbers are good or bad?

384. Can they use the already stated?

385. Account for the make-or-buy process and how to perform the financial calculations involved in the process. What are the main types of contracts if you do decide to outsource?

386. Does a process exist to identify individuals authorized to make certain decisions?

387. What are the main parts of a scope statement?

388. Would you rate yourself as being risk-averse, risk-neutral, or risk-seeking?

389. Consider the examples of poor quality in

information technology Loyalty Program projects presented in the What Went Wrong?

390. What time management activity should you do NEXT?

391. What steps did your organization take to earn this prestigious quality award?

392. Why is it difficult to use Loyalty Program project management software well?

393. What is the shortest possible time it will take to complete this Loyalty Program project?

394. Do an internet search on earning pmp certification. be sure to search for yahoo groups related to this topic. what are the options you found to help people prepare for the exam?

395. What type of people would you want on your team?

396. How does poking fun at technical professionals communications skills impact the industry and educational programs?

397. Are activity dependencies identified?

398. Which best describes how this affects the Loyalty Program project?

399. Is a Loyalty Program project charter created once a Loyalty Program project is formally recognized?

2.18 Duration Estimating Worksheet: Loyalty Program

400. Does the Loyalty Program project provide innovative ways for stakeholders to overcome obstacles or deliver better outcomes?

401. What work will be included in the Loyalty Program project?

402. What is next?

403. What is your role?

404. What is cost and Loyalty Program project cost management?

405. What info is needed?

406. Why estimate time and cost?

407. Is this operation cost effective?

408. Is the Loyalty Program project responsive to community need?

409. Is a construction detail attached (to aid in explanation)?

410. Done before proceeding with this activity or what can be done concurrently?

411. When, then?

412. Do any colleagues have experience with your organization and/or RFPs?

413. What questions do you have?

414. What utility impacts are there?

415. How can the Loyalty Program project be displayed graphically to better visualize the activities?

416. When do the individual activities need to start and finish?

417. Will the Loyalty Program project collaborate with the local community and leverage resources?

2.19 Project Schedule: Loyalty Program

418. How can you address that situation?

419. Should you have a test for each code module?

420. Did the Loyalty Program project come in on schedule?

421. What is the difference?

422. Why is software Loyalty Program project disaster so common?

423. Are key risk mitigation strategies added to the Loyalty Program project schedule?

424. How do you manage Loyalty Program project Risk?

425. Is there a Schedule Management Plan that establishes the criteria and activities for developing, monitoring and controlling the Loyalty Program project schedule?

426. Are there activities that came from a template or previous Loyalty Program project that are not applicable on this phase of this Loyalty Program project?

427. Did the Loyalty Program project come in under budget?

428. Understand the constraints used in preparing the schedule. Are activities connected because logic dictates the order in which others occur?

429. Did the final product meet or exceed user expectations?

430. To what degree is do you feel the entire team was committed to the Loyalty Program project schedule?

431. What is Loyalty Program project management?

432. How can you minimize or control changes to Loyalty Program project schedules?

433. What does that mean?

434. How effectively were issues able to be resolved without impacting the Loyalty Program project Schedule or Budget?

2.20 Cost Management Plan: Loyalty Program

435. Is stakeholder involvement adequate?

436. Is the Loyalty Program project schedule available for all Loyalty Program project team members to review?

437. Is your organization certified as a supplier, wholesaler, regular dealer, or manufacturer of corresponding products/supplies?

438. What would you do differently what did not work?

439. Have process improvement efforts been completed before requirements efforts begin?

440. Are risk triggers captured?

441. Timeline and milestones?

442. Is it possible to track all classes of Loyalty Program project work (e.g. scheduled, un-scheduled, defect repair, etc.)?

443. Are changes in deliverable commitments agreed to by all affected groups & individuals?

444. Cost management – how will the cost of changes be estimated and controlled?

445. Have lessons learned been conducted after each Loyalty Program project release?

446. Are vendor contract reports, reviews and visits conducted periodically?

447. Has the budget been baselined?

448. Is the communication plan being followed?

449. Eac -estimate at completion, what is the total job expected to cost?

450. Will the forecasts be based on trend analysis and earned value statistics?

451. Are changes in scope (deliverable commitments) agreed to by all affected groups & individuals?

452. Are all vendor contracts closed out?

2.21 Activity Cost Estimates: Loyalty Program

453. Were the tasks or work products prepared by the consultant useful?

454. Does the activity rely on a common set of tools to carry it out?

455. What cost data should be used to estimate costs during the 2-year follow-up period?

456. What areas does the group agree are the biggest success on the Loyalty Program project?

457. Would you hire them again?

458. Will you use any tools, such as Loyalty Program project management software, to assist in capturing Earned Value metrics?

459. How quickly can the task be done with the skills available?

460. Who determines when the contractor is paid?

461. Vac -variance at completion, how much over/under budget do you expect to be?

462. Can you delete activities or make them inactive?

463. What is the last item a Loyalty Program project manager must do to finalize Loyalty Program project

close-out?

464. Certification of actual expenditures?

465. Where can you get activity reports?

466. Maintenance Reserve?

467. What defines a successful Loyalty Program project?

468. What are you looking for?

469. Specific - is the objective clear in terms of what, how, when, and where the situation will be changed?

470. Does the estimator have experience?

471. Does the estimator estimate by task or by person?

2.22 Cost Estimating Worksheet: Loyalty Program

472. Identify the timeframe necessary to monitor progress and collect data to determine how the selected measure has changed?

473. Value pocket identification & quantification what are value pockets?

474. Who is best positioned to know and assist in identifying corresponding factors?

475. What additional Loyalty Program project(s) could be initiated as a result of this Loyalty Program project?

476. Can a trend be established from historical performance data on the selected measure and are the criteria for using trend analysis or forecasting methods met?

477. What is the estimated labor cost today based upon this information?

478. Will the Loyalty Program project collaborate with the local community and leverage resources?

479. What costs are to be estimated?

480. Is it feasible to establish a control group arrangement?

481. What can be included?

482. Ask: are others positioned to know, are others credible, and will others cooperate?

483. What is the purpose of estimating?

484. What will others want?

485. Is the Loyalty Program project responsive to community need?

486. How will the results be shared and to whom?

487. Does the Loyalty Program project provide innovative ways for stakeholders to overcome obstacles or deliver better outcomes?

488. What happens to any remaining funds not used?

2.23 Cost Baseline: Loyalty Program

489. What deliverables come first?

490. Are procedures defined by which the cost baseline may be changed?

491. What weaknesses do you have?

492. How fast?

493. What does a good WBS NOT look like?

494. Is the cr within Loyalty Program project scope?

495. On budget?

496. Verify business objectives. Are others appropriate, and well-articulated?

497. Have all approved changes to the cost baseline been identified and impact on the Loyalty Program project documented?

498. Are you asking management for something as a result of this update?

499. How will cost estimates be used?

500. Does a process exist for establishing a cost baseline to measure Loyalty Program project performance?

501. Have all the product or service deliverables been

accepted by the customer?

502. Has the appropriate access to relevant data and analysis capability been granted?

503. Impact to environment?

504. Loyalty Program project goals -should others be reconsidered?

505. Have you identified skills that are missing from your team?

506. What threats might prevent you from getting there?

507. What is cost and Loyalty Program project cost management?

2.24 Quality Management Plan: Loyalty Program

508. How relevant is this attribute to this Loyalty Program project or audit?

509. Do trained quality assurance auditors conduct the audits as defined in the Quality Management Plan and scheduled by the Loyalty Program project manager?

510. What are the appropriate test methods to be used?

511. What is quality and how will you ensure it?

512. Does the system design reflect the requirements?

513. How is staff trained?

514. Are there procedures in place to effectively manage interdependencies with other Loyalty Program projects / systems?

515. What are your results for key measures/indicators of accomplishment of organizational strategy?

516. How are changes recorded?

517. Is it necessary?

518. How are records kept in the office?

519. What process do you use to minimize errors, defects, and rework?

520. What type of in-house testing do you conduct?

521. Diagrams and tables to account for complex concepts and increase overall readability?

522. Show/provide copy of procedures for taking field notes?

523. What data do you gather/use/compile?

524. What worked well?

2.25 Quality Metrics: Loyalty Program

525. Subjective quality component: customer satisfaction, how do you measure it?

526. Filter visualizations of interest?

527. Is there a set of procedures to capture, analyze and act on quality metrics?

528. Which are the right metrics to use?

529. Was review conducted per standard protocols?

530. What can manufacturing professionals do to ensure quality is seen as an integral part of the entire product lifecycle?

531. What forces exist that would cause them to change?

532. What are you trying to accomplish?

533. Should a modifier be included?

534. Are applicable standards referenced and available?

535. Are documents on hand to provide explanations of privacy and confidentiality?

536. What metrics do you measure?

537. How do you know if everyone is trying to

improve the right things?

538. Are there any open risk issues?

539. Which data do others need in one place to target areas of improvement?

540. What is the benchmark?

541. How is it being measured?

542. Is a risk containment plan in place?

543. Product Availability ?

544. Are quality metrics defined?

2.26 Process Improvement Plan: Loyalty Program

545. Where do you want to be?

546. What personnel are the champions for the initiative?

547. Have the supporting tools been developed or acquired?

548. Does explicit definition of the measures exist?

549. Does your process ensure quality?

550. Why quality management?

551. Why do you want to achieve the goal?

552. Has a process guide to collect the data been developed?

553. What personnel are the sponsors for that initiative?

554. Who should prepare the process improvement action plan?

555. What personnel are the change agents for your initiative?

556. Where are you now?

557. What actions are needed to address the problems and achieve the goals?

558. What lessons have you learned so far?

559. Modeling current processes is great, and will you ever see a return on that investment?

560. To elicit goal statements, do you ask a question such as, What do you want to achieve?

561. Are you making progress on the goals?

2.27 Responsibility Assignment Matrix: Loyalty Program

562. What expertise is available in your department?

563. Are the wbs and organizational levels for application of the Loyalty Program projected overhead costs identified?

564. How do you assist them to be as productive as possible?

565. Identify and isolate causes of favorable and unfavorable cost and schedule variances?

566. Are authorized changes being incorporated in a timely manner?

567. Are the bases and rates for allocating costs from each indirect pool consistently applied?

568. Contemplated overhead expenditure for each period based on the best information currently available?

569. Cwbs elements to be subcontracted, with identification of subcontractors?

570. Are records maintained to show how management reserves are used?

571. Are material costs reported within the same period as that in which BCWP is earned for that

material?

572. Changes in the direct base to which overhead costs are allocated?

573. All cwbs elements specified for external reporting?

574. Are the actual costs used for variance analysis reconcilable with data from the accounting system?

575. What do you do when people do not respond?

576. Changes in the current direct and Loyalty Program projected base?

577. Detailed schedules which support control account and work package start and completion dates/events?

578. Are people afraid to let you know when others are under allocated?

2.28 Roles and Responsibilities: Loyalty Program

579. Implementation of actions: Who are the responsible units?

580. What should you highlight for improvement?

581. How well did the Loyalty Program project Team understand the expectations of specific roles and responsibilities?

582. Are your budgets supportive of a culture of quality data?

583. Are the quality assurance functions and related roles and responsibilities clearly defined?

584. Do you take the time to clearly define roles and responsibilities on Loyalty Program project tasks?

585. Does the team have access to and ability to use data analysis tools?

586. How is your work-life balance?

587. Accountabilities: what are the roles and responsibilities of individual team members?

588. What expectations were met?

589. What is working well?

590. Is feedback clearly communicated and non-judgmental?

591. What specific behaviors did you observe?

592. Attainable / achievable: the goal is attainable; can you actually accomplish the goal?

593. What are your major roles and responsibilities in the area of performance measurement and assessment?

594. Was the expectation clearly communicated?

595. Is there a training program in place for stakeholders covering expectations, roles and responsibilities and any addition knowledge others need to be good stakeholders?

596. What areas of supervision are challenging for you?

597. Are Loyalty Program project team roles and responsibilities identified and documented?

2.29 Human Resource Management Plan: Loyalty Program

598. Has a structured approach been used to break work effort into manageable components (WBS)?

599. Has a resource management plan been created?

600. Have adequate resources been provided by management to ensure Loyalty Program project success?

601. Were the budget estimates reasonable?

602. Is current scope of the Loyalty Program project substantially different than that originally defined?

603. Have Loyalty Program project management standards and procedures been identified / established and documented?

604. Are status reports received per the Loyalty Program project Plan?

605. Is the quality assurance team identified?

606. Are corrective actions and variances reported?

607. Quality of people required to meet the forecast needs of the department?

608. Staffing Requirements?

609. What areas does the group agree are the biggest success on the Loyalty Program project?

610. Have external dependencies been captured in the schedule?

611. How are superior performers differentiated from average performers?

612. Do people have the competencies to meet the strategic objectives?

613. Is there a formal process for updating the Loyalty Program project baseline?

614. Are adequate resources provided for the quality assurance function?

615. Has the Loyalty Program project scope been baselined?

2.30 Communications Management Plan: Loyalty Program

616. Who will use or be affected by the result of a Loyalty Program project?

617. Which stakeholders are thought leaders, influences, or early adopters?

618. Is there an important stakeholder who is actively opposed and will not receive messages?

619. Who is the stakeholder?

620. Who have you worked with in past, similar initiatives?

621. What is the political influence?

622. How much time does it take to do it?

623. Do you ask; can you recommend others for you to talk with about this initiative?

624. Who to share with?

625. Do you then often overlook a key stakeholder or stakeholder group?

626. What is the stakeholders level of authority?

627. Are others part of the communications management plan?

628. Are stakeholders internal or external?

629. What to know?

630. Who did you turn to if you had questions?

631. How often do you engage with stakeholders?

632. Are there potential barriers between the team and the stakeholder?

633. How is this initiative related to other portfolios, programs, or Loyalty Program projects?

634. What data is going to be required?

2.31 Risk Management Plan: Loyalty Program

635. Are you working on the right risks?

636. Is the customer willing to establish rapid communication links with the developer?

637. How well were you able to manage your risk before?

638. Are there alternative opinions/solutions/ processes you should explore?

639. Have top software and customer managers formally committed to support the Loyalty Program project?

640. Management -what contingency plans do you have if the risk becomes a reality?

641. Premium on reliability of product?

642. Financial risk: can your organization afford to undertake the Loyalty Program project?

643. Market risk -will the new service or product be useful to your organization or marketable to others?

644. What did not work so well?

645. Do you manage the process through use of metrics?

646. Are tools for analysis and design available?

647. Can you stabilize dynamic risk factors?

648. What would you do?

649. What are the cost, schedule and resource impacts if the risk does occur?

650. What does a risk management program do?

651. Prioritized components/features?

652. Are there new risks that mitigation strategies might introduce?

653. Is the number of people on the Loyalty Program project team adequate to do the job?

654. Is the technology to be built new to your organization?

2.32 Risk Register: Loyalty Program

655. Is further information required before making a decision?

656. Severity Prediction?

657. Technology risk -is the Loyalty Program project technically feasible?

658. What are the main aims, objectives of the policy, strategy, or service and the intended outcomes?

659. How could corresponding Risk affect the Loyalty Program project in terms of cost and schedule?

660. What is the appropriate level of risk management for this Loyalty Program project?

661. Are there other alternative controls that could be implemented?

662. What is a Community Risk Register?

663. Who is accountable?

664. How well are risks controlled?

665. Why would you develop a risk register?

666. Are your objectives at risk?

667. Budget and schedule: what are the estimated costs and schedules for performing risk-related

activities?

668. Risk documentation: what reporting formats and processes will be used for risk management activities?

669. What evidence do you have to justify the likelihood score of the risk (audit, incident report, claim, complaints, inspection, internal review)?

670. Who needs to know about this?

671. What are the major risks facing the Loyalty Program project?

672. Are there any gaps in the evidence?

673. What is the reason for current performance gaps and do the risks and opportunities identified previously account for this?

2.33 Probability and Impact Assessment: Loyalty Program

674. Are flexibility and reuse paramount?

675. How completely has the customer been identified?

676. Anticipated volatility of the requirements?

677. What is the likelihood?

678. Do the people have the right combinations of skills?

679. What risks are necessary to achieve success?

680. Risks should be identified during which phase of Loyalty Program project management life cycle?

681. Are tool mentors available?

682. What are the current demands of the customer?

683. Have customers been involved fully in the definition of requirements?

684. What will be the impact or consequence if the risk occurs?

685. What are the uncertainties associated with the technology selected for the Loyalty Program project?

686. Can this technology be absorbed with current level of expertise available in your organization?

687. Is security a central objective?

688. Risk categorization -which of your categories has more risk than others?

689. What risks does your organization have if the Loyalty Program projects fail to meet deadline?

690. Do the requirements require the creation of new algorithms?

691. Supply/demand Loyalty Program projections and trends; what are the levels of accuracy?

692. What are the chances the risk event will occur?

2.34 Probability and Impact Matrix: Loyalty Program

693. Which is the BEST thing to do?

694. Does the customer have a solid idea of what is required?

695. What things are likely to change?

696. What will be the likely political situation during the life of the Loyalty Program project?

697. What are the current requirements of the customer?

698. Who should be notified of the occurrence of each of the risk indicators?

699. What should be the level of coordination?

700. What is the impact if the risk does occur?

701. How do you define a risk?

702. How carefully have the potential competitors been identified?

703. Who has experience with this?

704. Who are the owners?

705. How would you assess the risk management

process in the Loyalty Program project?

706. What should you do FIRST?

707. Could others have been better mitigated?

708. Lay ground work for future returns?

709. What are data sources?

710. Are the risk data complete?

711. Are you on schedule?

2.35 Risk Data Sheet: Loyalty Program

712. What can you do?

713. What are you weak at and therefore need to do better?

714. What do you know?

715. What is the environment within which you operate (social trends, economic, community values, broad based participation, national directions etc.)?

716. What were the Causes that contributed?

717. How reliable is the data source?

718. Will revised controls lead to tolerable risk levels?

719. What are you here for (Mission)?

720. What actions can be taken to eliminate or remove risk?

721. Potential for recurrence?

722. How can hazards be reduced?

723. What is the likelihood of it happening?

724. What are your core values?

725. Are new hazards created?

726. During work activities could hazards exist?

727. Is the data sufficiently specified in terms of the type of failure being analyzed, and its frequency or probability?

728. What is the chance that it will happen?

729. Has the most cost-effective solution been chosen?

730. What are the main threats to your existence?

2.36 Procurement Management Plan: Loyalty Program

731. Is there a Quality Management Plan?

732. Is the assigned Loyalty Program project manager a PMP (Certified Loyalty Program project manager) and experienced?

733. Is the schedule updated on a periodic basis?

734. Were sponsors and decision makers available when needed outside regularly scheduled meetings?

735. Were Loyalty Program project team members involved in the development of activity & task decomposition?

736. What types of contracts will be used?

737. Is there a Steering Committee in place?

738. Are action items captured and managed?

739. Are the Loyalty Program project team members located locally to the users/stakeholders?

740. Have activity relationships and interdependencies within tasks been adequately identified?

741. Are written status reports provided on a designated frequent basis?

742. Based on your Loyalty Program project communication management plan, what worked well?

743. How and when do you enter into Loyalty Program project Procurement Management?

744. Does the resource management plan include a personnel development plan?

745. Is the structure for tracking the Loyalty Program project schedule well defined and assigned to a specific individual?

746. Is a pmo (Loyalty Program project management office) in place which provides oversight to the Loyalty Program project?

747. Are schedule deliverables actually delivered?

748. Do you have the reasons why the changes to your organizational systems and capabilities are required?

749. Have adequate resources been provided by management to ensure Loyalty Program project success?

750. Are governance roles and responsibilities documented?

2.37 Source Selection Criteria: Loyalty Program

751. Will the technical evaluation factor unnecessarily force the acquisition into a higher-priced market segment?

752. Can you prevent comparison of proposals?

753. Have all evaluators been trained?

754. How will you evaluate offerors proposals?

755. Comparison of each offers prices to the estimated prices -are there significant differences?

756. What will you use to capture evaluation and subsequent documentation?

757. Who must be notified?

758. How much past performance information should be requested?

759. How do you facilitate evaluation against published criteria?

760. What information may not be provided?

761. How organization are proposed quotes/prices?

762. How should oral presentations be prepared for?

763. How can solicitation Schedules be improved to yield more effective price competition?

764. What procedures are followed when a contractor requires access to classified information or a significant quantity of special material/information?

765. What are the most common types of rating systems?

766. Are there any specific considerations that precludes offers from being selected as the awardee?

767. What should communications be used to accomplish?

768. What are the steps in performing a cost/tech tradeoff?

769. What evidence should be provided regarding proposal evaluations?

770. How can business terms and conditions be improved to yield more effective price competition?

2.38 Stakeholder Management Plan: Loyalty Program

771. What inspection and testing is to be performed?

772. Detail warranty and/or maintenance periods?

773. Do any protocols apply for records management?

774. Is it standard practice to formally commit stakeholders to the Loyalty Program project via agreements?

775. Are tasks tracked by hours?

776. Are there any potential occupational health and safety issues due to the proposed purchases?

777. Do you use diagrams and tables to account for complex concepts and increase overall readability?

778. Contradictory information between different documents?

779. Are stakeholders aware and supportive of the principles and practices of modern software estimation?

780. Are Loyalty Program project leaders committed to this Loyalty Program project full time?

781. Has the Loyalty Program project manager been identified?

782. What information should be collected?

783. Have the procedures for identifying budget variances been followed?

784. Have key stakeholders been identified?

785. Have all stakeholders been identified?

786. Are metrics used to evaluate and manage Vendors?

787. Are non-critical path items updated and agreed upon with the teams?

788. Is there an onboarding process in place?

2.39 Change Management Plan: Loyalty Program

789. What are the responsibilities assigned to each role?

790. What is the worst thing that can happen if you chose not to communicate this information?

791. Will a different work structure focus people on what is important?

792. Are work location changes required?

793. How much change management is needed?

794. What is going to be done differently?

795. What time commitment will this involve?

796. Why would a Loyalty Program project run more smoothly when change management is emphasized from the beginning?

797. When should a given message be communicated?

798. Is it the same for each of the business units?

799. Has a training need analysis been carried out?

800. How do you gain sponsors buy-in to the communication plan?

801. Will the culture embrace or reject this change?

802. What are you trying to achieve as a result of communication?

803. Who will fund the training?

804. How frequently should you repeat the message?

805. How does the principle of senders and receivers make the Loyalty Program project communications effort more complex?

806. Where will the funds come from?

807. Does this change represent a completely new process for your organization, or a different application of an existing process?

3.0 Executing Process Group: Loyalty Program

808. What are deliverables of your Loyalty Program project?

809. Just how important is your work to the overall success of the Loyalty Program project?

810. What is the difference between conceptual, application, and evaluative questions?

811. What are the main parts of the scope statement?

812. Do the partners have sufficient financial capacity to keep up the benefits produced by the programme?

813. What were things that you did well, and could improve, and how?

814. What are the critical steps involved with strategy mapping?

815. What are the main processes included in Loyalty Program project quality management?

816. On which process should team members spend the most time?

817. How well did the chosen processes produce the expected results?

818. How can you use Microsoft Loyalty Program

project and Excel to assist in Loyalty Program project risk management?

819. Why should Loyalty Program project managers strive to make jobs look easy?

820. Do the products created live up to the necessary quality?

821. Who are the Loyalty Program project stakeholders?

822. How does Loyalty Program project management relate to other disciplines?

823. Are the necessary foundations in place to ensure the sustainability of the results of the programme?

824. Are decisions made in a timely manner?

825. When is the appropriate time to bring the scorecard to Board meetings?

3.1 Team Member Status Report: Loyalty Program

826. What is to be done?

827. Why is it to be done?

828. How much risk is involved?

829. Are your organizations Loyalty Program projects more successful over time?

830. Does every department have to have a Loyalty Program project Manager on staff?

831. How can you make it practical?

832. Does your organization have the means (staff, money, contract, etc.) to produce or to acquire the product, good, or service?

833. What specific interest groups do you have in place?

834. Will the staff do training or is that done by a third party?

835. When a teams productivity and success depend on collaboration and the efficient flow of information, what generally fails them?

836. Are the products of your organizations Loyalty Program projects meeting customers objectives?

837. How does this product, good, or service meet the needs of the Loyalty Program project and your organization as a whole?

838. Does the product, good, or service already exist within your organization?

839. The problem with Reward & Recognition Programs is that the truly deserving people all too often get left out. How can you make it practical?

840. Is there evidence that staff is taking a more professional approach toward management of your organizations Loyalty Program projects?

841. How will resource planning be done?

842. Are the attitudes of staff regarding Loyalty Program project work improving?

843. Do you have an Enterprise Loyalty Program project Management Office (EPMO)?

844. How it is to be done?

3.2 Change Request: Loyalty Program

845. Will all change requests and current status be logged?

846. What must be taken into consideration when introducing change control programs?

847. What is a Change Request Form?

848. Has a formal technical review been conducted to assess technical correctness?

849. How many times must the change be modified or presented to the change control board before it is approved?

850. Will the change use memory to the extent that other functions will be not have sufficient memory to operate effectively?

851. When do you create a change request?

852. Have all related configuration items been properly updated?

853. What is the relationship between requirements attributes and attributes like complexity and size?

854. Can you answer what happened, who did it, when did it happen, and what else will be affected?

855. Which requirements attributes affect the risk to reliability the most?

856. Will there be a change request form in use?

857. How is quality being addressed on the Loyalty Program project?

858. Are you implementing itil processes?

859. How is the change documented (format, content, storage)?

860. Has the change been highlighted and documented in the CSCI?

861. What is the relationship between requirements attributes and reliability?

862. How can you ensure that changes have been made properly?

863. How are the measures for carrying out the change established?

864. Who is included in the change control team?

3.3 Change Log: Loyalty Program

865. When was the request submitted?

866. Is the change backward compatible without limitations?

867. How does this relate to the standards developed for specific business processes?

868. Is the submitted change a new change or a modification of a previously approved change?

869. Where do changes come from?

870. Is the change request open, closed or pending?

871. Who initiated the change request?

872. Do the described changes impact on the integrity or security of the system?

873. Is this a mandatory replacement?

874. How does this change affect scope?

875. Is the change request within Loyalty Program project scope?

876. Does the suggested change request represent a desired enhancement to the products functionality?

877. Should a more thorough impact analysis be conducted?

878. When was the request approved?

879. Will the Loyalty Program project fail if the change request is not executed?

880. Is the requested change request a result of changes in other Loyalty Program project(s)?

881. How does this change affect the timeline of the schedule?

882. Does the suggested change request seem to represent a necessary enhancement to the product?

3.4 Decision Log: Loyalty Program

883. How do you know when you are achieving it?

884. Who will be given a copy of this document and where will it be kept?

885. Is your opponent open to a non-traditional workflow, or will it likely challenge anything you do?

886. Adversarial environment. is your opponent open to a non-traditional workflow, or will it likely challenge anything you do?

887. How does the use a Decision Support System influence the strategies/tactics or costs?

888. It becomes critical to track and periodically revisit both operational effectiveness; Are you noticing all that you need to, and are you interpreting what you see effectively?

889. What are the cost implications?

890. Does anything need to be adjusted?

891. Is everything working as expected?

892. Which variables make a critical difference?

893. How do you define success?

894. What makes you different or better than others companies selling the same thing?

895. How consolidated and comprehensive a story can you tell by capturing currently available incident data in a central location and through a log of key decisions during an incident?

896. How does an increasing emphasis on cost containment influence the strategies and tactics used?

897. Behaviors; what are guidelines that the team has identified that will assist them with getting the most out of team meetings?

898. Who is the decisionmaker?

899. At what point in time does loss become unacceptable?

900. Do strategies and tactics aimed at less than full control reduce the costs of management or simply shift the cost burden?

901. What is your overall strategy for quality control / quality assurance procedures?

902. What is the line where eDiscovery ends and document review begins?

3.5 Quality Audit: Loyalty Program

903. How does your organization know whether they are adhering to mission and achieving objectives?

904. How does your organization know that its relationships with relevant professional bodies are appropriately effective and constructive?

905. How does your organization know that the support for its staff is appropriately effective and constructive?

906. How does your organization know that the range and quality of its accommodation, catering and transportation services are appropriately effective and constructive?

907. Are there appropriate indicators for monitoring the effectiveness and efficiency of processes?

908. What is your organizations greatest strength?

909. How does your organization know that its planning processes are appropriately effective and constructive?

910. Will the evidence likely be sufficient and appropriate?

911. Does the audit organization have experience in performing the required work for entities of your type and size?

912. Is your organizations resource allocation system properly aligned with its collection of intentions?

913. How does your organization know that its systems for communicating with and among staff are appropriately effective and constructive?

914. How does your organization know that its research programs are appropriately effective and constructive?

915. Are adequate and conveniently located toilet facilities available for use by the employees?

916. How does your organization know that its staff placements are appropriately effective and constructive in relation to program-related learning outcomes?

917. How does your organization know that its Governance system is appropriately effective and constructive?

918. How do you know what, specifically, is required of you in your work?

919. How does your organization know that its staff entrance standards are appropriately effective and constructive and being implemented consistently?

920. Is there a written corporate quality policy?

921. What are the main things that hinder your ability to do a good job?

922. Is there any content that may be legally

actionable?

3.6 Team Directory: Loyalty Program

923. Who should receive information (all stakeholders)?

924. Process decisions: do job conditions warrant additional actions to collect job information and document on-site activity?

925. Who are the Team Members?

926. Process decisions: which organizational elements and which individuals will be assigned management functions?

927. How does the team resolve conflicts and ensure tasks are completed?

928. Who will write the meeting minutes and distribute?

929. Who will report Loyalty Program project status to all stakeholders?

930. Where will the product be used and/or delivered or built when appropriate?

931. Timing: when do the effects of communication take place?

932. Process decisions: how well was task order work performed?

933. Who will be the stakeholders on your next

Loyalty Program project?

934. Why is the work necessary?

935. Decisions: is the most suitable form of contract being used?

936. Who will talk to the customer?

937. When will you produce deliverables?

938. Process decisions: are contractors adequately prosecuting the work?

939. Process decisions: do invoice amounts match accepted work in place?

940. How and in what format should information be presented?

941. Process decisions: are there any statutory or regulatory issues relevant to the timely execution of work?

942. When does information need to be distributed?

3.7 Team Operating Agreement: Loyalty Program

943. What administrative supports will be put in place to support the team and the teams supervisor?

944. Do you call or email participants to ensure understanding, follow-through and commitment to the meeting outcomes?

945. What are the safety issues/risks that need to be addressed and/or that the team needs to consider?

946. Do you brief absent members after they view meeting notes or listen to a recording?

947. Did you delegate tasks such as taking meeting minutes, presenting a topic and soliciting input?

948. Are there the right people on your team?

949. Conflict resolution: how will disputes and other conflicts be mediated or resolved?

950. What is the number of cases currently teamed?

951. Are leadership responsibilities shared among team members (versus a single leader)?

952. Reimbursements: how will the team members be reimbursed for expenses and time commitments?

953. To whom do you deliver your services?

954. What types of accommodations will be formulated and put in place for sustaining the team?

955. What resources can be provided for the team in terms of equipment, space, time for training, protected time and space for meetings, and travel allowances?

956. Do team members need to frequently communicate as a full group to make timely decisions?

957. Have you set the goals and objectives of the team?

958. Communication protocols: how will the team communicate?

959. Do you send out the agenda and meeting materials in advance?

960. What is the anticipated procedure (recruitment, solicitation of volunteers, or assignment) for selecting team members?

961. Are there more than two national cultures represented by your team?

962. Do you leverage technology engagement tools group chat, polls, screen sharing, etc.?

3.8 Team Performance Assessment: Loyalty Program

963. What makes opportunities more or less obvious?

964. Delaying market entry: how long is too long?

965. To what degree does the teams work approach provide opportunity for members to engage in fact-based problem solving?

966. To what degree does the teams work approach provide opportunity for members to engage in results-based evaluation?

967. To what degree are the teams goals and objectives clear, simple, and measurable?

968. To what degree are the members clear on what they are individually responsible for and what they are jointly responsible for?

969. To what degree is there a sense that only the team can succeed?

970. To what degree do members articulate the goals beyond the team membership?

971. To what degree will the team ensure that all members equitably share the work essential to the success of the team?

972. To what degree are the relative importance and

priority of the goals clear to all team members?

973. Lack of method variance in self-reported affect and perceptions at work: Reality or artifact?

974. Can team performance be reliably measured in simulator and live exercises using the same assessment tool?

975. If you have criticized someones work for method variance in your role as reviewer, what was the circumstance?

976. Social categorization and intergroup behaviour: Does minimal intergroup discrimination make social identity more positive?

977. How much interpersonal friction is there in your team?

978. If you have received criticism from reviewers that your work suffered from method variance, what was the circumstance?

979. To what degree does the teams work approach provide opportunity for members to engage in open interaction?

980. When does the medium matter?

981. To what degree are corresponding categories of skills either actually or potentially represented across the membership?

982. To what degree is the team cognizant of small wins to be celebrated along the way?

3.9 Team Member Performance Assessment: Loyalty Program

983. How do you determine which data are the most important to use, analyze, or review?

984. What makes them effective?

985. Why do performance reviews?

986. To what degree are the goals ambitious?

987. To what degree can the team measure progress against specific goals?

988. To what degree does the team possess adequate membership to achieve its ends?

989. What future plans (e.g., modifications) do you have for your program?

990. How should adaptive assessments be implemented?

991. Are the draft goals SMART ?

992. How is performance assessment used in making future award decisions including options and extend/compete decisions?

993. What is the role of the Reviewer?

994. Who they are?

995. What is a general description of the processes under performance measurement and assessment?

996. What are top priorities?

997. Are the goals SMART ?

998. Are any governance changes sufficient to impact achievement?

999. Where can team members go for more detailed information on performance measurement and assessment?

1000. What are they responsible for?

1001. To what extent did the evaluation influence the instructional path, such as with adaptive testing?

3.10 Issue Log: Loyalty Program

1002. Are there too many who have an interest in some aspect of your work?

1003. Is the issue log kept in a safe place?

1004. Why do you manage communications?

1005. In classifying stakeholders, which approach to do so are you using?

1006. Is access to the Issue Log controlled?

1007. What is the status of the issue?

1008. Why multiple evaluators?

1009. Do you often overlook a key stakeholder or stakeholder group?

1010. How were past initiatives successful?

1011. Are the Loyalty Program project issues uniquely identified, including to which product they refer?

1012. Where do team members get information?

1013. Which team member will work with each stakeholder?

1014. What would have to change?

1015. What steps can you take for positive

relationships?

1016. Which stakeholders can influence others?

1017. Do you feel a register helps?

1018. What date was the issue resolved?

1019. What is a Stakeholder?

4.0 Monitoring and Controlling Process Group: Loyalty Program

1020. Is the verbiage used appropriate and understandable?

1021. User: who wants the information and what are they interested in?

1022. Is there sufficient funding available for this?

1023. Is the program in place as intended?

1024. How to ensure validity, quality and consistency?

1025. What input will you be required to provide the Loyalty Program project team?

1026. How were collaborations developed, and how are they sustained?

1027. How will staff learn how to use the deliverables?

1028. Where is the Risk in the Loyalty Program project?

1029. Were decisions made in a timely manner?

1030. Purpose: toward what end is the evaluation being conducted?

1031. Feasibility: how much money, time, and effort can you put into this?

1032. Accuracy: what design will lead to accurate information?

1033. Is the program making progress in helping to achieve the set results?

1034. How is agile portfolio management done?

1035. When will the Loyalty Program project be done?

1036. How was the program set-up initiated?

4.1 Project Performance Report: Loyalty Program

1037. To what degree are the structures of the formal organization consistent with the behaviors in the informal organization?

1038. To what degree will each member have the opportunity to advance his or her professional skills in all three of the above categories while contributing to the accomplishment of the teams purpose and goals?

1039. To what degree can the cognitive capacity of individuals accommodate the flow of information?

1040. To what degree do team members feel that the purpose of the team is important, if not exciting?

1041. What is in it for you?

1042. To what degree do the goals specify concrete team work products?

1043. To what degree are the skill areas critical to team performance present?

1044. To what degree does the task meet individual needs?

1045. To what degree are the goals realistic?

1046. To what degree do team members understand one anothers roles and skills?

1047. To what degree are fresh input and perspectives systematically caught and added (for example, through information and analysis, new members, and senior sponsors)?

1048. To what degree do the structures of the formal organization motivate taskrelevant behavior and facilitate task completion?

1049. To what degree is there centralized control of information sharing?

1050. To what degree can the team ensure that all members are individually and jointly accountable for the teams purpose, goals, approach, and work-products?

1051. To what degree do team members agree with the goals, relative importance, and the ways in which achievement will be measured?

1052. To what degree will new and supplemental skills be introduced as the need is recognized?

1053. To what degree does the teams purpose contain themes that are particularly meaningful and memorable?

4.2 Variance Analysis: Loyalty Program

1054. How does the monthly budget compare to the actual experience?

1055. Contract line items and end items?

1056. Why do variances exist?

1057. Are the wbs and organizational levels for application of the Loyalty Program projected overhead costs identified?

1058. How do you evaluate the impact of schedule changes, work around, et?

1059. What does a favorable labor efficiency variance mean?

1060. Are procedures for variance analysis documented and consistently applied at the control account level and selected WBS and organizational levels at least monthly as a routine task?

1061. Is there a logical explanation for any variance?

1062. Favorable or unfavorable variance?

1063. Is cost and schedule performance measurement done in a consistent, systematic manner?

1064. Are estimates of costs at completion generated

in a rational, consistent manner?

1065. What is the total budget for the Loyalty Program project (including estimates for authorized and unpriced work)?

1066. Does the contractors system include procedures for measuring the performance of critical subcontractors?

1067. Are work packages assigned to performing organizations?

1068. Are all elements of indirect expense identified to overhead cost budgets of Loyalty Program projections?

1069. Are there changes in the direct base to which overhead costs are allocated?

1070. Who are responsible for the establishment of budgets and assignment of resources for overhead performance?

1071. Is budgeted cost for work performed calculated in a manner consistent with the way work is planned?

1072. What are the actual costs to date?

4.3 Earned Value Status: Loyalty Program

1073. Are you hitting your Loyalty Program projects targets?

1074. Verification is a process of ensuring that the developed system satisfies the stakeholders agreements and specifications; Are you building the product right? What do you verify?

1075. If earned value management (EVM) is so good in determining the true status of a Loyalty Program project and Loyalty Program project its completion, why is it that hardly any one uses it in information systems related Loyalty Program projects?

1076. Where is evidence-based earned value in your organization reported?

1077. How does this compare with other Loyalty Program projects?

1078. How much is it going to cost by the finish?

1079. Earned value can be used in almost any Loyalty Program project situation and in almost any Loyalty Program project environment. it may be used on large Loyalty Program projects, medium sized Loyalty Program projects, tiny Loyalty Program projects (in cut-down form), complex and simple Loyalty Program projects and in any market sector. some people, of course, know all about earned value, they have used it for years - but perhaps not as effectively as they could have?

1080. When is it going to finish?

1081. Validation is a process of ensuring that the developed system will actually achieve the stakeholders desired outcomes; Are you building the right product? What do you validate?

1082. Where are your problem areas?

1083. What is the unit of forecast value?

4.4 Risk Audit: Loyalty Program

1084. Which assets are important?

1085. Is risk an management agenda item?

1086. Do you have written and signed agreements/ contracts in place for each paid staff member?

1087. Does the Loyalty Program project team have experience with the technology to be implemented?

1088. Are auditors able to effectively apply more soft evidence found in the risk-assessment process with the results of more tangible audit evidence found through more substantive testing?

1089. Are the best people available?

1090. Can analytical tests provide evidence that is as strong as evidence from traditional substantive tests?

1091. Do you ensure the recommended rules of play and protocols are followed for your activity?

1092. What risk does not having unique identification present?

1093. Is your organization willing to commit significant time to the requirements gathering process?

1094. How do you manage risk?

1095. Tradeoff: how much risk can be tolerated and still deliver the products where they need to be?

1096. Will an appropriate standard of care be applied to all involved?

1097. Should additional substantive testing be conducted because of the risk audit results?

1098. Strategic business risk audit methodologies; are corresponding an attempt to sell other services, and is management becoming the client of the audit rather than the shareholder?

1099. Will safety checks of personal equipment supplied by competitors be conducted?

1100. Do industry specialists and business risk auditors enhance audit reporting accuracy?

1101. For this risk .. what do you need to stop doing, start doing and keep doing?

4.5 Contractor Status Report: Loyalty Program

1102. Describe how often regular updates are made to the proposed solution. Are corresponding regular updates included in the standard maintenance plan?

1103. What was the budget or estimated cost for your organizations services?

1104. Who can list a Loyalty Program project as organization experience, your organization or a previous employee of your organization?

1105. What was the overall budget or estimated cost?

1106. Are there contractual transfer concerns?

1107. How does the proposed individual meet each requirement?

1108. What is the average response time for answering a support call?

1109. What was the actual budget or estimated cost for your organizations services?

1110. What process manages the contracts?

1111. If applicable; describe your standard schedule for new software version releases. Are new software version releases included in the standard maintenance plan?

1112. How long have you been using the services?

1113. What was the final actual cost?

1114. What are the minimum and optimal bandwidth requirements for the proposed solution?

1115. How is risk transferred?

4.6 Formal Acceptance: Loyalty Program

1116. Did the Loyalty Program project manager and team act in a professional and ethical manner?

1117. Was the Loyalty Program project work done on time, within budget, and according to specification?

1118. Was the Loyalty Program project goal achieved?

1119. Does it do what Loyalty Program project team said it would?

1120. Did the Loyalty Program project achieve its MOV?

1121. Who would use it?

1122. What features, practices, and processes proved to be strengths or weaknesses?

1123. What are the requirements against which to test, Who will execute?

1124. How well did the team follow the methodology?

1125. What was done right?

1126. Is formal acceptance of the Loyalty Program project product documented and distributed?

1127. Does it do what client said it would?

1128. General estimate of the costs and times to complete the Loyalty Program project?

1129. What lessons were learned about your Loyalty Program project management methodology?

1130. Do you perform formal acceptance or burn-in tests?

1131. Was the sponsor/customer satisfied?

1132. Do you buy pre-configured systems or build your own configuration?

1133. Was business value realized?

1134. Was the Loyalty Program project managed well?

1135. Who supplies data?

5.0 Closing Process Group: Loyalty Program

1136. What areas does the group agree are the biggest success on the Loyalty Program project?

1137. Are there funding or time constraints?

1138. Does the close educate others to improve performance?

1139. Did you do things well?

1140. Based on your Loyalty Program project communication management plan, what worked well?

1141. Did the Loyalty Program project team have the right skills?

1142. Were escalated issues resolved promptly?

1143. Is this a follow-on to a previous Loyalty Program project?

1144. Just how important is your work to the overall success of the Loyalty Program project?

1145. How well defined and documented were the Loyalty Program project management processes you chose to use?

1146. Were the outcomes different from the already

stated planned?

1147. Will the Loyalty Program project deliverable(s) replace a current asset or group of assets?

1148. Did the delivered product meet the specified requirements and goals of the Loyalty Program project?

1149. Did the Loyalty Program project team have enough people to execute the Loyalty Program project plan?

1150. What were things that you did very well and want to do the same again on the next Loyalty Program project?

1151. What do you need to do?

1152. Was the user/client satisfied with the end product?

5.1 Procurement Audit: Loyalty Program

1153. Do the employees have the necessary skills and experience to carry out procurements efficiently?

1154. Do at least two people have custodial responsibilities for negotiable checks (one checking on the other)?

1155. Is the opportunity properly published?

1156. Did you consider and evaluate alternatives, like bundling needs with other departments or grouping supplies in separate lots with different characteristics?

1157. Was all the key documentation given to the contracting authority?

1158. Are fixed asset accounts posted currently?

1159. Are all purchase orders reviewed by someone other than the individual preparing the purchase order (reasonableness of order and vendor selection)?

1160. Were the tender documents comprehensive, transparent and free from restrictions or conditions which would discriminate against certain suppliers?

1161. Is there a need for the procurement Loyalty Program project at all?

1162. Where applicable, did your organization

adequately manage experts employed to assist in the procurement process?

1163. Budget controls: does your organization maintain an up-to-date (approved) budget for all funded activities, and perform a comparison of that budget with actual expenditures for each budget category?

1164. Does an appropriately qualified official check the quality of performance against the contract terms?

1165. Are eu procurement regulations applicable?

1166. Were any additional works or deliveries admissible without the need for a new procurement procedure?

1167. Is the chosen supplier part of your organizations database?

1168. Does the procurement function/unit have the ability to negotiate with customers and suppliers?

1169. Are approval limits definitive as to amount and classification of expenditure?

1170. Are staff members evaluated in accordance with the terms of existing negotiated agreements?

1171. Is the procurement function/unit organized the most appropriate way taking into consideration the actual tasks which the department has to carry out?

1172. Do appropriate controls ensure that

procurement decisions are not biased by conflicts of interest or corruption?

5.2 Contract Close-Out: Loyalty Program

1173. Was the contract type appropriate?

1174. Parties: Authorized?

1175. Change in circumstances?

1176. Why Outsource?

1177. What happens to the recipient of services?

1178. How/when used ?

1179. Have all contract records been included in the Loyalty Program project archives?

1180. Has each contract been audited to verify acceptance and delivery?

1181. Have all contracts been closed?

1182. Have all acceptance criteria been met prior to final payment to contractors?

1183. Change in knowledge?

1184. Was the contract complete without requiring numerous changes and revisions?

1185. Change in attitude or behavior?

1186. How does it work?

1187. Was the contract sufficiently clear so as not to result in numerous disputes and misunderstandings?

1188. What is capture management?

1189. Are the signers the authorized officials?

1190. Have all contracts been completed?

1191. Parties: who is involved?

1192. How is the contracting office notified of the automatic contract close-out?

5.3 Project or Phase Close-Out: Loyalty Program

1193. What are they?

1194. What is the information level of detail required for each stakeholder?

1195. What were the desired outcomes?

1196. How often did each stakeholder need an update?

1197. What was expected from each stakeholder?

1198. What stakeholder group needs, expectations, and interests are being met by the Loyalty Program project?

1199. Were risks identified and mitigated?

1200. When and how were information needs best met?

1201. What information did each stakeholder need to contribute to the Loyalty Program projects success?

1202. What are the informational communication needs for each stakeholder?

1203. Complete yes or no?

1204. Does the lesson educate others to improve

performance?

1205. In preparing the Lessons Learned report, should it reflect a consensus viewpoint, or should the report reflect the different individual viewpoints?

1206. What is a Risk Management Process?

1207. Is the lesson significant, valid, and applicable?

1208. Planned remaining costs?

1209. What can you do better next time, and what specific actions can you take to improve?

1210. What could have been improved?

1211. Which changes might a stakeholder be required to make as a result of the Loyalty Program project?

5.4 Lessons Learned: Loyalty Program

1212. How effective were your functional specs?

1213. How adaptable is the deliverable?

1214. Was there enough support – guidance, clerical support, training?

1215. What would you like to see better documented about how to use existing processes on this type of Loyalty Program project?

1216. Who had fiscal authority to manage the funding for the Loyalty Program project, did that work?

1217. Was Loyalty Program project performance validated or challenged?

1218. Were the right people available when required?

1219. What is your working hypothesis, if you have one?

1220. Was sufficient time allocated to review Loyalty Program project deliverables?

1221. What is the frequency of group communications?

1222. Were the Loyalty Program project objectives met (if not, briefly account for what wasnt met)?

1223. What were the most significant issues on this

Loyalty Program project?

1224. How effective were Loyalty Program project audits?

1225. What was the methodology behind successful learning experiences, and how might they be applied to the broader challenge of your organizations knowledge management?

1226. What Loyalty Program project circumstances were not anticipated?

1227. How satisfied are you with your involvement in the development and/or review of the Loyalty Program project Scope during Loyalty Program project Initiation and Planning?

1228. Who has execution authority?

1229. How much of your time was spent on other than this Loyalty Program project?

1230. What were the challenges and pitfalls?

Loyalty Program and Managing Projects, Criteria for Project Managers:

1.0 Initiating Process Group: Loyalty Program

1. Does it make any difference if you am successful?

2. Are the Loyalty Program project team and stakeholders meeting regularly and using a meeting agenda and taking notes to accurately document what is being covered and what happened in the weekly meetings?

3. Does the Loyalty Program project team have enough people to execute the Loyalty Program project plan?

4. Are identified risks being monitored properly, are new risks arising during the Loyalty Program project or are foreseen risks occurring?

5. What communication items need improvement?

6. If the risk event occurs, what will you do?

7. How will you know you did it?

8. What do they need to know about the Loyalty Program project?

9. How will it affect me?

10. What were things that you need to improve?

11. What were the challenges that you encountered during the execution of a previous Loyalty Program project that you would not want to repeat?

12. What technical work to do in each phase?

13. What input will you be required to provide the Loyalty Program project team?

14. Do you know all the stakeholders impacted by the Loyalty Program project and what needs are?

15. In which Loyalty Program project management process group is the detailed Loyalty Program project budget created?

16. Were sponsors and decision makers available when needed outside regularly scheduled meetings?

17. Information sharing?

18. Who does what?

19. Do you understand the quality and control criteria that must be achieved for successful Loyalty Program project completion?

20. The Loyalty Program project you are managing has nine stakeholders. How many channel of communications are there between corresponding stakeholders?

1.1 Project Charter: Loyalty Program

21. How much?

22. Avoid costs, improve service, and/ or comply with a mandate?

23. Why executive support?

24. How are Loyalty Program projects different from operations?

25. What is the business need?

26. What is the most common tool for helping define the detail?

27. How will you know a change is an improvement?

28. Must Have?

29. Who ise input and support will this Loyalty Program project require?

30. Who manages integration?

31. What are the assumptions?

32. Why have you chosen the aim you have set forth?

33. When is a charter needed?

34. What changes can you make to improve?

35. When do you use a Loyalty Program project Charter?

36. Why Outsource?

37. Fit with other Products Compliments – Cannibalizes?

38. Customer benefits: what customer requirements does this Loyalty Program project address?

39. Who will take notes, document decisions?

1.2 Stakeholder Register: Loyalty Program

40. What are the major Loyalty Program project milestones requiring communications or providing communications opportunities?

41. How should employers make voices heard?

42. Who is managing stakeholder engagement?

43. How much influence do they have on the Loyalty Program project?

44. Who are the stakeholders?

45. Is your organization ready for change?

46. What opportunities exist to provide communications?

47. What is the power of the stakeholder?

48. How big is the gap?

49. How will reports be created?

50. What & Why?

51. Who wants to talk about Security?

1.3 Stakeholder Analysis Matrix: Loyalty Program

52. Who has control over whom?

53. Business and product development?

54. What mechanisms are proposed to monitor and measure Loyalty Program project performance in terms of social development outcomes?

55. Industry or lifestyle trends?

56. Are you working on the right risks?

57. What makes a person a stakeholder?

58. Inoculations or payment to receive them?

59. Why do you care?

60. Legislative effects?

61. Insurmountable weaknesses?

62. Continuity, supply chain robustness?

63. Will the impacts be local, national or international?

64. What do people from other organizations see as your organizations weaknesses?

65. Management cover, succession?

66. Are the required specifications for products or services changing?

67. How can you counter negative efforts?

68. What is relationship with the Loyalty Program project?

69. How do you manage Loyalty Program project Risk?

70. Marketing - reach, distribution, awareness?

71. What do people from other organizations see as your strengths?

2.0 Planning Process Group: Loyalty Program

72. Contingency planning. if a risk event occurs, what will you do?

73. Is the Loyalty Program project making progress in helping to achieve the set results?

74. Are there efficient coordination mechanisms to avoid overloading the counterparts, participating stakeholders?

75. If action is called for, what form should it take?

76. Who are the Loyalty Program project stakeholders?

77. What do you need to do?

78. How should needs be met?

79. Do the partners have sufficient financial capacity to keep up the benefits produced by the programme?

80. On which process should team members spend the most time?

81. To what extent has the intervention strategy been adapted to the areas of intervention in which it is being implemented?

82. To what extent are the visions and actions of the partners consistent or divergent with regard to the

program?

83. What do they need to know about the Loyalty Program project?

84. You are creating your WBS and find that you keep decomposing tasks into smaller and smaller units. How can you tell when you are done?

85. Is the schedule for the set products being met?

86. Did the program design/ implementation strategy adequately address the planning stage necessary to set up structures, hire staff etc.?

87. Will the products created live up to the necessary quality?

88. What will you do?

89. Why is it important to determine activity sequencing on Loyalty Program projects?

90. How will you do it?

2.1 Project Management Plan: Loyalty Program

91. What is risk management?

92. What did not work so well?

93. Who is the sponsor?

94. Are alternatives safe, functional, constructible, economical, reasonable and sustainable?

95. What are the training needs?

96. If the Loyalty Program project is complex or scope is specialized, do you have appropriate and/or qualified staff available to perform the tasks?

97. Why do you manage integration?

98. Is the budget realistic?

99. What happened during the process that you found interesting?

100. What would you do differently what did not work?

101. What are the deliverables?

102. Will you add a schedule and diagram?

103. How well are you able to manage your risk?

104. Why Change?

105. How can you best help your organization to develop consistent practices in Loyalty Program project management planning stages?

106. What worked well?

107. Are the existing and future without-plan conditions reasonable and appropriate?

108. Do the proposed changes from the Loyalty Program project include any significant risks to safety?

109. Are there any Client staffing expectations?

110. Is mitigation authorized or recommended?

2.2 Scope Management Plan: Loyalty Program

111. Are any non-compliance issues that exist due to organizations practices?

112. Has appropriate allowance been made for the effect of the learning curve on all personnel joining the Loyalty Program project who do not have the required prior industry, functional & technical expertise?

113. Organizational policies that might affect the availability of resources?

114. Is your organization structure for both tracking & controlling the budget well defined and assigned to a specific individual?

115. Who is responsible for monitoring the Loyalty Program project scope to ensure the Loyalty Program project remains within the scope baseline?

116. Can the Loyalty Program project team do several activities in parallel?

117. Have reserves been created to address risks?

118. Is the Loyalty Program project sponsor clearly communicating the business case or rationale for why this Loyalty Program project is needed?

119. How much money have you spent?

120. What are the Quality Assurance overheads?

121. Will anyone else be involved in verifying the deliverables?

122. Deliverables -are the deliverables tangible and verifiable?

123. Is there any form of automated support for Issues Management?

124. Are the results of quality assurance reviews provided to affected groups & individuals?

125. Are you meeting with stake holders and team members?

126. Was the scope definition used in task sequencing?

127. Where do scope processes fit in?

128. Is stakeholder involvement adequate?

129. Are enough systems & user personnel assigned to the Loyalty Program project?

130. Timeline and milestones?

2.3 Requirements Management Plan: Loyalty Program

131. Do you understand the role that each stakeholder will play in the requirements process?

132. How often will the reporting occur?

133. Define the help desk model. who will take full responsibility?

134. What are you counting on?

135. Is stakeholder risk tolerance an important factor for the requirements process in this Loyalty Program project?

136. Controlling Loyalty Program project requirements involves monitoring the status of the Loyalty Program project requirements and managing changes to the requirements. Who is responsible for monitoring and tracking the Loyalty Program project requirements?

137. Is the user satisfied?

138. Who has the authority to reject Loyalty Program project requirements?

139. In case of software development; Should you have a test for each code module?

140. Subject to change control?

141. Who will finally present the work or product(s) for acceptance?

142. Have stakeholders been instructed in the Change Control process?

143. Do you have price sheets and a methodology for determining the total proposal cost?

144. Do you have an appropriate arrangement for meetings?

145. Will you document changes to requirements?

146. Do you know which stakeholders will participate in the requirements effort?

147. Do you expect stakeholders to be cooperative?

148. How will you develop the schedule of requirements activities?

149. Is it new or replacing an existing business system or process?

150. Do you have an agreed upon process for alerting the Loyalty Program project Manager if a request for change in requirements leads to a product scope change?

2.4 Requirements Documentation: Loyalty Program

151. Are there any requirements conflicts?

152. How does the proposed Loyalty Program project contribute to the overall objectives of your organization?

153. Is your business case still valid?

154. What kind of entity is a problem ?

155. What facilities must be supported by the system?

156. What will be the integration problems?

157. Where do you define what is a customer, what are the attributes of customer?

158. Do your constraints stand?

159. What are the acceptance criteria?

160. What marketing channels do you want to use: e-mail, letter or sms?

161. How will they be documented / shared?

162. Consistency. are there any requirements conflicts?

163. How much testing do you need to do to prove

that your system is safe?

164. How much does requirements engineering cost?

165. What happens when requirements are wrong?

166. Where are business rules being captured?

167. What is your Elevator Speech?

168. Is the requirement realistically testable?

169. Do technical resources exist?

170. Can you check system requirements?

2.5 Requirements Traceability Matrix: Loyalty Program

171. What are the chronologies, contingencies, consequences, criteria?

172. Why do you manage scope?

173. How small is small enough?

174. Describe the process for approving requirements so they can be added to the traceability matrix and Loyalty Program project work can be performed. Will the Loyalty Program project requirements become approved in writing?

175. Do you have a clear understanding of all subcontracts in place?

176. Will you use a Requirements Traceability Matrix?

177. How will it affect the stakeholders personally in career?

178. What is the WBS?

179. Is there a requirements traceability process in place?

180. How do you manage scope?

181. What percentage of Loyalty Program projects are producing traceability matrices between

requirements and other work products?

182. Why use a WBS?

2.6 Project Scope Statement: Loyalty Program

183. Is there a process (test plans, inspections, reviews) defined for verifying outputs for each task?

184. Is the plan for Loyalty Program project resources adequate?

185. What went wrong?

186. Is the Loyalty Program project manager qualified and experienced in Loyalty Program project management?

187. If you were to write a list of what should not be included in the scope statement, what are the things that you would recommend be described as out-of-scope?

188. Elements that deal with providing the detail?

189. Relevant - ask yourself can you get there; why are you doing this Loyalty Program project?

190. Are the input requirements from the team members clearly documented and communicated?

191. How will you verify the accuracy of the work of the Loyalty Program project, and what constitutes acceptance of the deliverables?

192. What is change?

193. Are there specific processes you will use to evaluate and approve/reject changes?

194. Will statistics related to QA be collected, trends analyzed, and problems raised as issues?

195. Any new risks introduced or old risks impacted. Are there issues that could affect the existing requirements for the result, service, or product if the scope changes?

196. Are there completion/verification criteria defined for each task producing an output?

197. Is this process communicated to the customer and team members?

198. Are there backup strategies for key members of the Loyalty Program project?

199. Will tasks be marked complete only after QA has been successfully completed?

200. Is an issue management process documented and filed?

201. Will an issue form be in use?

2.7 Assumption and Constraint Log: Loyalty Program

202. Is staff trained on the software technologies that are being used on the Loyalty Program project?

203. Do documented requirements exist for all critical components and areas, including technical, business, interfaces, performance, security and conversion requirements?

204. Is the current scope of the Loyalty Program project substantially different than that originally defined in the approved Loyalty Program project plan?

205. Does the document/deliverable meet general requirements (for example, statement of work) for all deliverables?

206. Does the system design reflect the requirements?

207. Does a specific action and/or state that is known to violate security policy occur?

208. Have the scope, objectives, costs, benefits and impacts been communicated to all involved and/or impacted stakeholders and work groups?

209. What weaknesses do you have?

210. Model-building: what data-analytic strategies are useful when building proportional-hazards models?

211. Are processes for release management of new development from coding and unit testing, to integration testing, to training, and production defined and followed?

212. Is the amount of effort justified by the anticipated value of forming a new process?

213. Are there procedures in place to effectively manage interdependencies with other Loyalty Program projects / systems?

214. Is this process still needed?

215. Does the document/deliverable meet all requirements (for example, statement of work) specific to this deliverable?

216. What other teams / processes would be impacted by changes to the current process, and how?

217. Is the process working, and people are not executing in compliance of the process?

218. Does the Loyalty Program project have a formal Loyalty Program project Plan?

219. Has the approach and development strategy of the Loyalty Program project been defined, documented and accepted by the appropriate stakeholders?

220. Are there cosmetic errors that hinder readability and comprehension?

221. Diagrams and tables are included to account for complex concepts and increase overall readability?

2.8 Work Breakdown Structure: Loyalty Program

222. Why is it useful?

223. Is it still viable?

224. Is it a change in scope?

225. What is the probability of completing the Loyalty Program project in less that xx days?

226. Do you need another level?

227. How many levels?

228. How much detail?

229. When does it have to be done?

230. Is the work breakdown structure (wbs) defined and is the scope of the Loyalty Program project clear with assigned deliverable owners?

231. When do you stop?

232. Who has to do it?

233. What is the probability that the Loyalty Program project duration will exceed xx weeks?

234. Why would you develop a Work Breakdown Structure?

235. How big is a work-package?

236. Where does it take place?

237. How will you and your Loyalty Program project team define the Loyalty Program projects scope and work breakdown structure?

238. Can you make it?

239. When would you develop a Work Breakdown Structure?

240. What has to be done?

2.9 WBS Dictionary: Loyalty Program

241. Knowledgeable Loyalty Program projections of future performance?

242. Actual cost of work performed?

243. Can the contractor substantiate work package and planning package budgets?

244. Are estimates developed by Loyalty Program project personnel coordinated with the already stated responsible for overall management to determine whether required resources will be available according to revised planning?

245. Do procedures specify under what circumstances replanning of open work packages may occur, and the methods to be followed?

246. Does the contractors system description or procedures require that the performance measurement baseline plus management reserve equal the contract budget base?

247. Does the contractors system include procedures for measuring the performance of critical subcontractors?

248. Does the contractors system provide unit or lot costs when applicable?

249. Are retroactive changes to direct costs and indirect costs prohibited except for the correction of

errors and routine accounting adjustments?

250. Are budgets or values assigned to work packages and planning packages in terms of dollars, hours, or other measurable units?

251. Is the entire contract planned in time-phased control accounts to the extent practicable?

252. Are the bases and rates for allocating costs from each indirect pool consistently applied?

253. Is subcontracted work defined and identified to the appropriate subcontractor within the proper WBS element?

254. Does the sum of all work package budgets plus planning packages within control accounts equal the budgets assigned to the already stated control accounts?

255. Are the bases and rates for allocating costs from each indirect pool to commercial work consistent with the already stated used to allocate corresponding costs to Government contracts?

256. What is the goal?

257. Are direct or indirect cost adjustments being accomplished according to accounting procedures acceptable to us?

2.10 Schedule Management Plan: Loyalty Program

258. Sensitivity analysis?

259. Has your organization readiness assessment been conducted?

260. Has a Loyalty Program project Communications Plan been developed?

261. Are cause and effect determined for risks when they occur?

262. Is the schedule feasible and at what cost?

263. Are the primary and secondary schedule tools defined?

264. Are the people assigned to the Loyalty Program project sufficiently qualified?

265. What date will the task finish?

266. Is your organization certified as a broker of the products/supplies?

267. Are risk triggers captured?

268. What tools and techniques will be used to estimate activity resources?

269. Are Loyalty Program project leaders committed

to this Loyalty Program project full time?

270. Is there a formal set of procedures supporting Stakeholder Management?

271. Where is the scheduling tool and who has access to it to view it?

272. Are Loyalty Program project team members involved in detailed estimating and scheduling?

273. Are all activities captured and do they address all approved work scope in the Loyalty Program project baseline?

274. Is there an on-going process in place to monitor Loyalty Program project risks?

275. Have key stakeholders been identified?

276. Has a capability assessment been conducted?

277. What strengths do you have?

2.11 Activity List: Loyalty Program

278. When do the individual activities need to start and finish?

279. What is your organizations history in doing similar activities?

280. What is the probability the Loyalty Program project can be completed in xx weeks?

281. Are the required resources available or need to be acquired?

282. The wbs is developed as part of a joint planning session. and how do you know that youhave done this right?

283. How detailed should a Loyalty Program project get?

284. What went well?

285. How should ongoing costs be monitored to try to keep the Loyalty Program project within budget?

286. Is there anything planned that does not need to be here?

287. What went right?

288. What did not go as well?

289. When will the work be performed?

290. How will it be performed?

291. What is the total time required to complete the Loyalty Program project if no delays occur?

292. Where will it be performed?

293. How difficult will it be to do specific activities on this Loyalty Program project?

294. Can you determine the activity that must finish, before this activity can start?

295. What are the critical bottleneck activities?

2.12 Activity Attributes: Loyalty Program

296. How else could the items be grouped?

297. Where else does it apply?

298. Why?

299. Has management defined a definite timeframe for the turnaround or Loyalty Program project window?

300. How do you manage time?

301. What activity do you think you should spend the most time on?

302. Activity: fair or not fair?

303. What is missing?

304. What is the general pattern here?

305. Does your organization of the data change its meaning?

306. Were there other ways you could have organized the data to achieve similar results?

307. Resources to accomplish the work?

308. How many days do you need to complete the

work scope with a limit of X number of resources?

309. How much activity detail is required?

310. Can you re-assign any activities to another resource to resolve an over-allocation?

311. Are the required resources available?

2.13 Milestone List: Loyalty Program

312. Competitive advantages?

313. Describe the concept of the technology, product or service that will be or has been developed. How will it be used?

314. What are your competitors vulnerabilities?

315. When will the Loyalty Program project be complete?

316. Global influences?

317. Do you foresee any technical risks or developmental challenges?

318. How soon can the activity finish?

319. What has been done so far?

320. Environmental effects?

321. Sustaining internal capabilities?

322. What is the market for your technology, product or service?

323. Identify critical paths (one or more) and which activities are on the critical path?

324. Describe the industry you are in and the market growth opportunities. What is the market for your

technology, product or service?

325. It is to be a narrative text providing the crucial aspects of your Loyalty Program project proposal answering what, who, how, when and where?

2.14 Network Diagram: Loyalty Program

326. What job or jobs precede it?

327. Are you on time?

328. Review the logical flow of the network diagram. Take a look at which activities you have first and then sequence the activities. Do they make sense?

329. Can you calculate the confidence level?

330. What are the Major Administrative Issues?

331. What is the lowest cost to complete this Loyalty Program project in xx weeks?

332. What is the probability of completing the Loyalty Program project in less that xx days?

333. How confident can you be in your milestone dates and the delivery date?

334. What activities must follow this activity?

335. Are the gantt chart and/or network diagram updated periodically and used to assess the overall Loyalty Program project timetable?

336. Where do schedules come from?

337. Why must you schedule milestones, such as

reviews, throughout the Loyalty Program project?

338. What are the tools?

339. Which type of network diagram allows you to depict four types of dependencies?

340. What job or jobs follow it?

341. What activity must be completed immediately before this activity can start?

342. Will crashing x weeks return more in benefits than it costs?

343. Planning: who, how long, what to do?

344. What job or jobs could run concurrently?

2.15 Activity Resource Requirements: Loyalty Program

345. Why do you do that?

346. How do you handle petty cash?

347. Are there unresolved issues that need to be addressed?

348. What are constraints that you might find during the Human Resource Planning process?

349. Organizational Applicability?

350. What is the Work Plan Standard?

351. Other support in specific areas?

352. Which logical relationship does the PDM use most often?

353. Anything else?

354. When does monitoring begin?

355. How many signatures do you require on a check and does this match what is in your policy and procedures?

356. Do you use tools like decomposition and rolling-wave planning to produce the activity list and other outputs?

357. Time for overtime?

2.16 Resource Breakdown Structure: Loyalty Program

358. Any changes from stakeholders?

359. When do they need the information?

360. Who will use the system?

361. What defines a successful Loyalty Program project?

362. The list could probably go on, but, the thing that you would most like to know is, How long & How much?

363. What is the primary purpose of the human resource plan?

364. How difficult will it be to do specific activities on this Loyalty Program project?

365. What can you do to improve productivity?

366. Goals for the Loyalty Program project. What is each stakeholders desired outcome for the Loyalty Program project?

367. Who will be used as a Loyalty Program project team member?

368. What is Loyalty Program project communication management?

369. Which resources should be in the resource pool?

370. Who delivers the information?

371. Which resource planning tool provides information on resource responsibility and accountability?

372. Why do you do it?

373. What is the purpose of assigning and documenting responsibility?

374. Is predictive resource analysis being done?

2.17 Activity Duration Estimates: Loyalty Program

375. Does a process exist to determine the probability of risk events?

376. Are Loyalty Program project activities decomposed into manageable components to ensure expected management control?

377. Can they use the already stated?

378. What time management activity should you do NEXT?

379. Why is there a growing trend in outsourcing, especially in the government?

380. Does the case present a realistic scenario?

381. After changes are approved are Loyalty Program project documents updated and distributed?

382. What are the main types of contracts if you do decide to outsource?

383. Why do you need a good WBS to use Loyalty Program project management software?

384. Do you think many other organizations could apply this methodology, or does each organization need to create its own methodology?

385. Does a process exist to identify Loyalty Program project roles, responsibilities and reporting relationships?

386. Do an internet search on earning pmp certification. be sure to search for yahoo groups related to this topic. what are the options you found to help people prepare for the exam?

387. How can others help Loyalty Program project managers understand your organizational context for Loyalty Program projects?

388. What are the largest companies that provide information technology outsourcing services?

389. What are key inputs and outputs of the software?

390. How does poking fun at technical professionals communications skills impact the industry and educational programs?

2.18 Duration Estimating Worksheet: Loyalty Program

391. Can the Loyalty Program project be constructed as planned?

392. Define the work as completely as possible. What work will be included in the Loyalty Program project?

393. What utility impacts are there?

394. Why estimate time and cost?

395. Is this operation cost effective?

396. Small or large Loyalty Program project?

397. For other activities, how much delay can be tolerated?

398. What questions do you have?

399. What is the total time required to complete the Loyalty Program project if no delays occur?

400. What is your role?

401. Do any colleagues have experience with your organization and/or RFPs?

402. Why estimate costs?

403. What info is needed?

404. What is cost and Loyalty Program project cost management?

405. What work will be included in the Loyalty Program project?

406. How should ongoing costs be monitored to try to keep the Loyalty Program project within budget?

407. Value pocket identification & quantification what are value pockets?

408. Science = process: remember the scientific method?

2.19 Project Schedule: Loyalty Program

409. Your best shot for providing estimations how complex/how much work does the activity require?

410. Are the original Loyalty Program project schedule and budget realistic?

411. Schedule/cost recovery?

412. To what degree is do you feel the entire team was committed to the Loyalty Program project schedule?

413. Why do you think schedule issues often cause the most conflicts on Loyalty Program projects?

414. How do you manage Loyalty Program project Risk?

415. How do you use schedules?

416. Your Loyalty Program project management plan results in a Loyalty Program project schedule that is too long. If the Loyalty Program project network diagram cannot change and you have extra personnel resources, what is the BEST thing to do?

417. Why is software Loyalty Program project disaster so common?

418. What is risk?

419. Verify that the update is accurate. Are all remaining durations correct?

420. Why time management?

421. What is the purpose of a Loyalty Program project schedule?

422. What is the difference?

423. How does a Loyalty Program project get to be a year late ?

424. Was the Loyalty Program project schedule reviewed by all stakeholders and formally accepted?

425. Why or why not?

426. Activity charts and bar charts are graphical representations of a Loyalty Program project schedule ...how do they differ?

2.20 Cost Management Plan: Loyalty Program

427. Does the Loyalty Program project have a formal Loyalty Program project Charter?

428. Are milestone deliverables effectively tracked and compared to Loyalty Program project plan?

429. Are parking lot items captured?

430. How do you manage cost?

431. Weve met your goals?

432. Responsibilities – what is the split of responsibilities between the owner and contractors?

433. Eac -estimate at completion, what is the total job expected to cost?

434. Escalation criteria met?

435. The definition of the Loyalty Program project scope what needs to be accomplished?

436. Are action items captured and managed?

437. Is the communication plan being followed?

438. Do Loyalty Program project teams & team members report on status / activities / progress?

439. Are the quality tools and methods identified in the Quality Plan appropriate to the Loyalty Program project?

440. Owner, contractor, and subcontractors?

441. Is there a set of procedures defining the scope, procedures, and deliverables defining quality control?

442. Is pert / critical path or equivalent methodology being used?

443. Is there a formal process for updating the Loyalty Program project baseline?

444. Quality assurance overheads?

445. Are status reports received per the Loyalty Program project Plan?

2.21 Activity Cost Estimates: Loyalty Program

446. What skill level is required to do the job?

447. Were escalated issues resolved promptly?

448. How do you change activities?

449. How do you allocate indirect costs to activities?

450. What is a Loyalty Program project Management Plan?

451. How do you fund change orders?

452. What areas were overlooked on this Loyalty Program project?

453. Can you delete activities or make them inactive?

454. Measurable - are the targets measurable?

455. What makes a good activity description?

456. Based on your Loyalty Program project communication management plan, what worked well?

457. Does the estimator estimate by task or by person?

458. Can you change your activities?

459. What procedures are put in place regarding bidding and cost comparisons, if any?

460. Scope statement only direct or indirect costs as well?

461. How do you do activity recasts?

462. How Award?

463. How many activities should you have?

464. Padding is bad and contingencies are good. what is the difference?

2.22 Cost Estimating Worksheet: Loyalty Program

465. Ask: are others positioned to know, are others credible, and will others cooperate?

466. Identify the timeframe necessary to monitor progress and collect data to determine how the selected measure has changed?

467. Does the Loyalty Program project provide innovative ways for stakeholders to overcome obstacles or deliver better outcomes?

468. Can a trend be established from historical performance data on the selected measure and are the criteria for using trend analysis or forecasting methods met?

469. Will the Loyalty Program project collaborate with the local community and leverage resources?

470. What will others want?

471. What is the estimated labor cost today based upon this information?

472. Who is best positioned to know and assist in identifying corresponding factors?

473. How will the results be shared and to whom?

474. What can be included?

475. What is the purpose of estimating?

476. Is it feasible to establish a control group arrangement?

477. What costs are to be estimated?

478. Is the Loyalty Program project responsive to community need?

479. What happens to any remaining funds not used?

480. What additional Loyalty Program project(s) could be initiated as a result of this Loyalty Program project?

2.23 Cost Baseline: Loyalty Program

481. Review your risk triggers -have your risks changed?

482. What is the consequence?

483. Will the Loyalty Program project fail if the change request is not executed?

484. How concrete were original objectives?

485. Have the resources used by the Loyalty Program project been reassigned to other units or Loyalty Program projects?

486. Has operations management formally accepted responsibility for operating and maintaining the product(s) or service(s) delivered by the Loyalty Program project?

487. Are you meeting with your team regularly?

488. What threats might prevent you from getting there?

489. What is the reality?

490. Vac -variance at completion, how much over/ under budget do you expect to be?

491. What is cost and Loyalty Program project cost management?

492. What would the life cycle costs be?

493. Has the documentation relating to operation and maintenance of the product(s) or service(s) been delivered to, and accepted by, operations management?

494. Is the cr within Loyalty Program project scope?

495. How long are you willing to wait before you find out were late?

496. How accurate do cost estimates need to be?

497. Are procedures defined by which the cost baseline may be changed?

498. Should a more thorough impact analysis be conducted?

2.24 Quality Management Plan: Loyalty Program

499. Written by multiple authors and in multiple writing styles?

500. How does your organization measure customer satisfaction/dissatisfaction?

501. How does your organization perform analyzes to assess overall organizational performance and set priorities?

502. Are requirements management tracking tools and procedures in place?

503. How does your organization recruit, hire, and retain new employees?

504. What would you gain if you spent time working to improve this process?

505. How is staff informed of proper reporting methods?

506. Are formal code reviews conducted?

507. Who is responsible for approving the qapp?

508. Were the right locations/samples tested for the right parameters?

509. Who do you send data to?

510. Was trending evident between reviews?

511. What are the appropriate test methods to be used?

512. What is the return on investment?

513. How are new requirements or changes to requirements identified?

514. How does your organization design processes to ensure others meet customer and others requirements?

515. Are there trends or hot spots?

516. How are senior leaders, employees, and your organization involved in supporting the community?

517. Sampling part of task?

518. How are changes to procedures made?

2.25 Quality Metrics: Loyalty Program

519. Is there a set of procedures to capture, analyze and act on quality metrics?

520. Have alternatives been defined in the event that failure occurs?

521. What level of statistical confidence do you use?

522. How does one achieve stability?

523. Why is now the time for quality metrics?

524. Do you know how much profit a 10% decrease in waste would generate?

525. What do you measure?

526. Are there any open risk issues?

527. Can visual measures help you to filter visualizations of interest?

528. What documentation is required?

529. Subjective quality component: customer satisfaction, how do you measure it?

530. What is the CMS Benchmark?

531. What if the biggest risk to your business were the already stated people who do not complain?

532. How should customers provide input?

533. Is a risk containment plan in place?

534. Which data do others need in one place to target areas of improvement?

535. Has trace of defects been initiated?

536. How effective are your security tests?

537. How can the effectiveness of each of the activities be measured?

2.26 Process Improvement Plan: Loyalty Program

538. Does your process ensure quality?

539. Does explicit definition of the measures exist?

540. How do you manage quality?

541. What lessons have you learned so far?

542. What is quality and how will you ensure it?

543. Have the supporting tools been developed or acquired?

544. Has the time line required to move measurement results from the points of collection to databases or users been established?

545. Why quality management?

546. Where do you focus?

547. Everyone agrees on what process improvement is, right?

548. Are you making progress on the improvement framework?

549. The motive is determined by asking, Why do you want to achieve this goal?

550. Modeling current processes is great, and will you ever see a return on that investment?

551. Management commitment at all levels?

552. Have the frequency of collection and the points in the process where measurements will be made been determined?

553. Are there forms and procedures to collect and record the data?

554. Are you following the quality standards?

555. What actions are needed to address the problems and achieve the goals?

556. Where do you want to be?

2.27 Responsibility Assignment Matrix: Loyalty Program

557. Evaluate the impact of schedule changes, work around, etc?

558. When performing is split among two or more roles, is the work clearly defined so that the efforts are coordinated and the communication is clear?

559. Is work progressively subdivided into detailed work packages as requirements are defined?

560. Budgeted cost for work scheduled?

561. Too many rs: with too many people labeled as doing the work, are there too many hands involved?

562. Are indirect costs accumulated for comparison with the corresponding budgets?

563. What expertise is not available in your department?

564. Budgets assigned to control accounts?

565. Who is the Loyalty Program project Manager?

566. Does the accounting system provide a basis for auditing records of direct costs chargeable to the contract?

567. Ideas for developing soft skills at your

organization?

568. Will too many Signing-off responsibilities delay the completion of the activity/deliverable?

569. Are the requirements for all items of overhead established by rational, traceable processes?

570. Budgets assigned to major functional organizations?

571. Is every signing-off responsibility and every communicating responsibility critically necessary?

572. Does the scheduling system identify in a timely manner the status of work?

573. Are meaningful indicators identified for use in measuring the status of cost and schedule performance?

574. If a role has only Signing-off, or only Communicating responsibility and has no Performing, Accountable, or Monitoring responsibility, is it necessary?

2.28 Roles and Responsibilities: Loyalty Program

575. Be specific; avoid generalities. Thank you and great work alone are insufficient. What exactly do you appreciate and why?

576. What should you do now to ensure that you are meeting all expectations of your current position?

577. Who: who is involved?

578. Is the data complete?

579. How is your work-life balance?

580. Attainable / achievable: the goal is attainable; can you actually accomplish the goal?

581. What areas of supervision are challenging for you?

582. Does the team have access to and ability to use data analysis tools?

583. Who is involved?

584. Where are you most strong as a supervisor?

585. What areas would you highlight for changes or improvements?

586. Concern: where are you limited or have no

authority, where you can not influence?

587. What should you highlight for improvement?

588. Influence: what areas of organizational decision making are you able to influence when you do not have authority to make the final decision?

589. What expectations were met?

590. Are governance roles and responsibilities documented?

591. Was the expectation clearly communicated?

592. Are your policies supportive of a culture of quality data?

593. Who is responsible for implementation activities and where will the functions, roles and responsibilities be defined?

2.29 Human Resource Management Plan: Loyalty Program

594. Do Loyalty Program project managers participating in the Loyalty Program project know the Loyalty Program projects true status first hand?

595. Has the Loyalty Program project scope been baselined?

596. Has a structured approach been used to break work effort into manageable components (WBS)?

597. Are all key components of a Quality Assurance Plan present?

598. What were things that you did well, and could improve, and how?

599. Specific - is the objective clear in terms of what, how, when, and where the situation will be changed?

600. Is it possible to track all classes of Loyalty Program project work (e.g. scheduled, un-scheduled, defect repair, etc.)?

601. Is the schedule updated on a periodic basis?

602. Are status reports received per the Loyalty Program project Plan?

603. Is there a formal set of procedures supporting Issues Management?

604. List the assumptions made to date. What did you have to assume to be true to complete the charter?

605. Is there an approved case?

606. What is the boss?

607. Are all payments made according to the contract(s)?

2.30 Communications Management Plan: Loyalty Program

608. Are there potential barriers between the team and the stakeholder?

609. What is the political influence?

610. What data is going to be required?

611. Why do you manage communications?

612. Who will use or be affected by the result of a Loyalty Program project?

613. Do you ask; can you recommend others for you to talk with about this initiative?

614. Is there an important stakeholder who is actively opposed and will not receive messages?

615. What is Loyalty Program project communications management?

616. What help do you and your team need from the stakeholder?

617. How were corresponding initiatives successful?

618. Do you prepare stakeholder engagement plans?

619. Are the stakeholders getting the information others need, are others consulted, are concerns

addressed?

620. Timing: when do the effects of the communication take place?

621. What is the stakeholders level of authority?

622. What are the interrelationships?

623. In your work, how much time is spent on stakeholder identification?

624. Are stakeholders internal or external?

625. Will messages be directly related to the release strategy or phases of the Loyalty Program project?

626. Are there too many who have an interest in some aspect of your work?

2.31 Risk Management Plan: Loyalty Program

627. Does the Loyalty Program project have the authority and ability to avoid the risk?

628. What is the impact to the Loyalty Program project if the item is not resolved in a timely fashion?

629. Which risks should get the attention?

630. How is risk monitoring performed?

631. Is security a central objective?

632. Are there risks to human health or the environment that need to be controlled or mitigated?

633. Financial risk -can your organization afford to undertake the Loyalty Program project?

634. Who/what can assist?

635. Do benefits and chances of success outweigh potential damage if success is not attained?

636. Does the Loyalty Program project team have experience with the technology to be implemented?

637. Is the necessary data being captured and is it complete and accurate?

638. How is the audit profession changing?

639. Do requirements demand the use of new analysis, design, or testing methods?

640. What will the damage be?

641. Are there new risks that mitigation strategies might introduce?

642. Can the Loyalty Program project proceed without assuming the risk?

643. What is the probability the risk avoidance strategy will be successful?

644. Have top software and customer managers formally committed to support the Loyalty Program project?

645. Can it be changed quickly?

646. Was an original risk assessment/risk management plan completed?

2.32 Risk Register: Loyalty Program

647. Contingency actions - planned actions to reduce the immediate seriousness of the risk when it does occur. What should you do when?

648. Preventative actions - planned actions to reduce the likelihood a risk will occur and/or reduce the seriousness should it occur. What should you do now?

649. What could prevent you delivering on the strategic program objectives and what is being done to mitigate corresponding issues?

650. Severity Prediction?

651. Risk categories: what are the main categories of risks that should be addressed on this Loyalty Program project?

652. Are there any knock-on effects/impact on any of the other areas?

653. How are risks graded?

654. Does the evidence highlight any areas to advance opportunities or foster good relations. If yes what steps will be taken?

655. How well are risks controlled?

656. Are corrective measures implemented as planned?

657. What should you do when?

658. Are implemented controls working as others should?

659. How are risks identified?

660. Methodology: how will risk management be performed on this Loyalty Program project?

661. What are you going to do to limit the Loyalty Program projects risk exposure due to the identified risks?

662. What is a Community Risk Register?

663. When is it going to be done?

664. Technology risk -is the Loyalty Program project technically feasible?

665. Who needs to know about this?

2.33 Probability and Impact Assessment: Loyalty Program

666. Is the process supported by tools?

667. How is the risk management process used in practice?

668. Have customers been involved fully in the definition of requirements?

669. Mitigation -how can you avoid the risk?

670. Does the software engineering team have the right mix of skills?

671. What is the risk appetite?

672. Who should be notified of the occurrence of each of the risk indicators?

673. Do the people have the right combinations of skills?

674. What will be cost of redeployment of personnel?

675. Is the Loyalty Program project cutting across the entire organization?

676. What is the experience (performance, attitude, business ethics, etc.) in the past with contractors?

677. Are the risk data timely and relevant?

678. What should be the level of coordination?

679. Can this technology be absorbed with current level of expertise available in your organization?

680. What are the industrial relations prevailing in your organization?

681. What should be the gestation period for the Loyalty Program project with specific technology?

682. How do the products attain the specifications?

683. How completely has the customer been identified?

2.34 Probability and Impact Matrix: Loyalty Program

684. Which role do you have in the Loyalty Program project?

685. What is the political situation at present?

686. Do the requirements require the creation of new algorithms?

687. What is the level of experience available with your organization?

688. What can you use the analyzed risks for?

689. How are the local factors going to affect the absorption?

690. Which phase of the Loyalty Program project do you take part in?

691. What is the industrial relations prevailing in this organization?

692. Are tool mentors available?

693. What should be the level of difficulty in handling the technology?

694. While preparing your risk responses, you identify additional risks. What should you do?

695. Do you manage the process through use of metrics?

696. How do risks change during the Loyalty Program projects life cycle?

697. What are the likely future requirements?

698. During Loyalty Program project executing, a team member identifies a risk that is not in the risk register. What should you do?

699. What are the risks involved in appointing external agencies to manage the Loyalty Program project?

700. Can you avoid altogether some things that might go wrong?

701. What are ways to measure and evaluate risks?

702. Has something like this been done before?

2.35 Risk Data Sheet: Loyalty Program

703. How do you handle product safely?

704. Whom do you serve (customers)?

705. Has a sensitivity analysis been carried out?

706. Potential for recurrence?

707. How can it happen?

708. What are you weak at and therefore need to do better?

709. What was measured?

710. Will revised controls lead to tolerable risk levels?

711. Are new hazards created?

712. Has the most cost-effective solution been chosen?

713. What were the Causes that contributed?

714. If it happens, what are the consequences?

715. What are the main threats to your existence?

716. Who has a vested interest in how you perform as your organization (our stakeholders)?

717. What can happen?

718. What are you trying to achieve (Objectives)?

2.36 Procurement Management Plan: Loyalty Program

719. Do you have the reasons why the changes to your organizational systems and capabilities are required?

720. Is there an issues management plan in place?

721. Have Loyalty Program project team accountabilities & responsibilities been clearly defined?

722. Why is procurement planning important?

723. Are multiple estimation methods being employed?

724. If standardized procurement documents are needed, where can others be found?

725. Are tasks tracked by hours?

726. Is a payment system in place with proper reviews and approvals?

727. Have all unresolved risks been documented?

728. What are your quality assurance overheads?

729. Alignment to strategic goals & objectives?

730. Has a resource management plan been created?

731. Is there a procurement management plan in place?

732. Is the assigned Loyalty Program project manager a PMP (Certified Loyalty Program project manager) and experienced?

733. Have adequate resources been provided by management to ensure Loyalty Program project success?

734. What areas are overlooked on this Loyalty Program project?

735. Has the scope management document been updated and distributed to help prevent scope creep?

736. Has Loyalty Program project success criteria been defined?

2.37 Source Selection Criteria: Loyalty Program

737. What information may not be provided?

738. In order of importance, which evaluation criteria are the most critical to the determination of your overall rating?

739. Do you prepare an independent cost estimate?

740. What should communications be used to accomplish?

741. Who is on the Source Selection Advisory Committee?

742. What should a DRFP include?

743. When must you conduct a debriefing?

744. What can not be disclosed?

745. Do you want to have them collaborate at subfactor level?

746. How should the oral presentations be handled?

747. Is the contracting office likely to receive more purchase requests for this item or service during the coming year?

748. Do you have designated specific forms or

worksheets?

749. Team leads: what is your process for assigning ratings?

750. When is it appropriate to issue a DRFP?

751. How are oral presentations documented?

752. Are they compliant with all technical requirements?

753. What is price analysis and when should it be performed?

754. Are there any specific considerations that precludes offers from being selected as the awardee?

755. How much past performance information should be requested?

756. What benefits are accrued from issuing a DRFP in advance of issuing a final RFP?

2.38 Stakeholder Management Plan: Loyalty Program

757. Have Loyalty Program project success criteria been defined?

758. How, to whom and how frequently will Risk status be reported?

759. Are staff skills known and available for each task?

760. Do any protocols apply for records management?

761. Have the procedures for identifying budget variances been followed?

762. Why is it important to reduce deliverables to a smallest component?

763. Are vendor invoices audited for accuracy before payment?

764. Is quality monitored from the perspective of the customers needs and expectations?

765. Have the key elements of a coherent Loyalty Program project management strategy been established?

766. Is there a requirements change management processes in place?

767. Is there a formal process for updating the Loyalty

Program project baseline?

768. Is there an onboarding process in place?

769. What guidelines or procedures currently exist that must be adhered to (eg departmental accounting procedures)?

770. How will the equipment be verified?

771. If a problem has been detected, what tools can be used to determine a root cause?

772. Have all necessary approvals been obtained?

773. Contradictory information between document sections?

774. Is the performance of the supplier to be rated and documented?

2.39 Change Management Plan: Loyalty Program

775. Impact of systems implementation on organization change?

776. What is going to be done differently?

777. How might they respond to the message and if the response may be negative or open to misinterpretation, what else needs to be said?

778. What new roles are needed?

779. What do you expect the target audience to do, say, think or feel as a result of this communication?

780. Who might be able to help you the most?

781. How many people are required in each of the roles?

782. Do you need a new organization structure?

783. Do the proposed users have access to the appropriate documentation?

784. Who might present the most resistance?

785. What is the reason for the communication?

786. What are the key change management success metrics?

787. What is the most positive interpretation it can receive?

788. What method and medium would you use to announce a message?

789. What are the training strategies?

790. What are the major changes to processes?

791. Is there a software application relevant to this deliverable?

792. What is the negative impact of communicating too soon or too late?

793. What new behaviours are required?

794. Are there any restrictions on who can receive the communications?

3.0 Executing Process Group: Loyalty Program

795. What areas were overlooked on this Loyalty Program project?

796. Just how important is your work to the overall success of the Loyalty Program project?

797. Do the products created live up to the necessary quality?

798. If a risk event occurs, what will you do?

799. What were things that you did very well and want to do the same again on the next Loyalty Program project?

800. After how many days will the lease cost be the same as the purchase cost for the equipment?

801. How does a Loyalty Program project life cycle differ from a product life cycle?

802. How well did the chosen processes fit the needs of the Loyalty Program project?

803. What are deliverables of your Loyalty Program project?

804. Will new hardware or software be required for servers or client machines?

805. What does it mean to take a systems view of a Loyalty Program project?

806. Is the Loyalty Program project making progress in helping to achieve the set results?

807. Who will provide training?

808. Do schedule issues conflicts?

809. What are the key components of the Loyalty Program project communications plan?

810. What are the Loyalty Program project management deliverables of each process group?

3.1 Team Member Status Report: Loyalty Program

811. Will the staff do training or is that done by a third party?

812. Does the product, good, or service already exist within your organization?

813. When a teams productivity and success depend on collaboration and the efficient flow of information, what generally fails them?

814. Are the products of your organizations Loyalty Program projects meeting customers objectives?

815. Does every department have to have a Loyalty Program project Manager on staff?

816. How will resource planning be done?

817. Why is it to be done?

818. What specific interest groups do you have in place?

819. Is there evidence that staff is taking a more professional approach toward management of your organizations Loyalty Program projects?

820. How it is to be done?

821. Are the attitudes of staff regarding Loyalty

Program project work improving?

822. How much risk is involved?

823. Does your organization have the means (staff, money, contract, etc.) to produce or to acquire the product, good, or service?

824. How does this product, good, or service meet the needs of the Loyalty Program project and your organization as a whole?

825. Do you have an Enterprise Loyalty Program project Management Office (EPMO)?

826. How can you make it practical?

827. The problem with Reward & Recognition Programs is that the truly deserving people all too often get left out. How can you make it practical?

828. What is to be done?

829. Are your organizations Loyalty Program projects more successful over time?

3.2 Change Request: Loyalty Program

830. How to get changes (code) out in a timely manner?

831. What is the function of the change control committee?

832. What is a Change Request Form?

833. Who can suggest changes?

834. Who needs to approve change requests?

835. Who is included in the change control team?

836. What mechanism is used to appraise others of changes that are made?

837. How is quality being addressed on the Loyalty Program project?

838. Why do you want to have a change control system?

839. What type of changes does change control take into account?

840. Have all related configuration items been properly updated?

841. Will the change use memory to the extent that other functions will be not have sufficient memory to operate effectively?

842. How are changes requested (forms, method of communication)?

843. How many lines of code must be changed to implement the change?

844. Can you answer what happened, who did it, when did it happen, and what else will be affected?

845. Will new change requests be acknowledged in a timely manner?

846. Will all change requests and current status be logged?

847. What has an inspector to inspect and to check?

848. How shall the implementation of changes be recorded?

849. What are the duties of the change control team?

3.3 Change Log: Loyalty Program

850. Is this a mandatory replacement?

851. Do the described changes impact on the integrity or security of the system?

852. Is the change request within Loyalty Program project scope?

853. Is the submitted change a new change or a modification of a previously approved change?

854. Where do changes come from?

855. When was the request approved?

856. When was the request submitted?

857. How does this change affect scope?

858. Is the change request open, closed or pending?

859. Who initiated the change request?

860. Does the suggested change request seem to represent a necessary enhancement to the product?

861. How does this change affect the timeline of the schedule?

862. Does the suggested change request represent a desired enhancement to the products functionality?

863. How does this relate to the standards developed for specific business processes?

864. Is the change backward compatible without limitations?

865. Is the requested change request a result of changes in other Loyalty Program project(s)?

866. Will the Loyalty Program project fail if the change request is not executed?

3.4 Decision Log: Loyalty Program

867. How do you define success?

868. Is your opponent open to a non-traditional workflow, or will it likely challenge anything you do?

869. Linked to original objective?

870. What is the line where eDiscovery ends and document review begins?

871. It becomes critical to track and periodically revisit both operational effectiveness; Are you noticing all that you need to, and are you interpreting what you see effectively?

872. Who is the decisionmaker?

873. Do strategies and tactics aimed at less than full control reduce the costs of management or simply shift the cost burden?

874. Meeting purpose; why does this team meet?

875. Which variables make a critical difference?

876. Behaviors; what are guidelines that the team has identified that will assist them with getting the most out of team meetings?

877. What is your overall strategy for quality control / quality assurance procedures?

878. What eDiscovery problem or issue did your organization set out to fix or make better?

879. Who will be given a copy of this document and where will it be kept?

880. What is the average size of your matters in an applicable measurement?

881. What makes you different or better than others companies selling the same thing?

882. How does an increasing emphasis on cost containment influence the strategies and tactics used?

883. Decision-making process; how will the team make decisions?

884. Adversarial environment. is your opponent open to a non-traditional workflow, or will it likely challenge anything you do?

885. How consolidated and comprehensive a story can you tell by capturing currently available incident data in a central location and through a log of key decisions during an incident?

886. How does provision of information, both in terms of content and presentation, influence acceptance of alternative strategies?

3.5 Quality Audit: Loyalty Program

887. Are people allowed to contribute ideas?

888. Does the audit organization have experience in performing the required work for entities of your type and size?

889. Is the process of self review, learning and improvement endemic throughout your organization?

890. How does your organization know that it is maintaining a conducive staff climate?

891. How do you indicate the extent to which your personnel would be expected to contribute to the work effort?

892. How does your organization know that its quality of teaching is appropriately effective and constructive?

893. How does your organization know that it is appropriately effective and constructive in preparing its staff for organizational aspirations?

894. Is there a written corporate quality policy?

895. What are your supplier audits?

896. How does your organization know that its planning processes are appropriately effective and constructive?

897. Are the policies and processes, as set out in the Quality Audit Manual, properly applied?

898. Are complaint files maintained?

899. Is progress against the intentions measurable?

900. What is your organizations greatest strength?

901. How does the organization know that its industry and community engagement planning and management systems are appropriately effective and constructive in enabling relationships with key stakeholder groups?

902. Do prior clients have a positive opinion of your organization?

903. Does your organization have set of goals, objectives, strategies and targets that are clearly understood by the Board and staff?

904. How does your organization know that its methods are appropriately effective and constructive?

905. How does your organization know that the system for managing its facilities is appropriately effective and constructive?

3.6 Team Directory: Loyalty Program

906. How and in what format should information be presented?

907. When does information need to be distributed?

908. How does the team resolve conflicts and ensure tasks are completed?

909. Who should receive information (all stakeholders)?

910. How will the team handle changes?

911. Process decisions: are contractors adequately prosecuting the work?

912. What are you going to deliver or accomplish?

913. Who are the Team Members?

914. Process decisions: are there any statutory or regulatory issues relevant to the timely execution of work?

915. Who will report Loyalty Program project status to all stakeholders?

916. Days from the time the issue is identified?

917. When will you produce deliverables?

918. Timing: when do the effects of communication

take place?

919. Process decisions: are all start-up, turn over and close out requirements of the contract satisfied?

920. Process decisions: which organizational elements and which individuals will be assigned management functions?

921. Where should the information be distributed?

922. Process decisions: is work progressing on schedule and per contract requirements?

3.7 Team Operating Agreement: Loyalty Program

923. Do you prevent individuals from dominating the meeting?

924. Must your members collaborate successfully to complete Loyalty Program projects?

925. Do you ensure that all participants know how to use the required technology?

926. Do you brief absent members after they view meeting notes or listen to a recording?

927. What resources can be provided for the team in terms of equipment, space, time for training, protected time and space for meetings, and travel allowances?

928. What individual strengths does each team member bring to the group?

929. To whom do you deliver your services?

930. How do you want to be thought of and known within your organization?

931. Is compensation based on team and individual performance?

932. What is the number of cases currently teamed?

933. How will you resolve conflict efficiently and respectfully?

934. How does teaming fit in with overall organizational goals and meet organizational needs?

935. Must your team members rely on the expertise of other members to complete tasks?

936. Why does your organization want to participate in teaming?

937. Reimbursements: how will the team members be reimbursed for expenses and time commitments?

938. What are the safety issues/risks that need to be addressed and/or that the team needs to consider?

939. What administrative supports will be put in place to support the team and the teams supervisor?

940. Does your team need access to all documents and information at all times?

941. Are leadership responsibilities shared among team members (versus a single leader)?

942. Do team members reside in more than two countries?

3.8 Team Performance Assessment: Loyalty Program

943. To what degree are the goals ambitious?

944. Is there a particular method of data analysis that you would recommend as a means of demonstrating that method variance is not of great concern for a given dataset?

945. What structural changes have you made or are you preparing to make?

946. Do you promptly inform members about major developments that may affect them?

947. How does Loyalty Program project termination impact Loyalty Program project team members?

948. To what degree are the relative importance and priority of the goals clear to all team members?

949. To what degree can the team measure progress against specific goals?

950. To what degree does the teams work approach provide opportunity for members to engage in results-based evaluation?

951. To what degree are the skill areas critical to team performance present?

952. To what degree can team members vigorously

define the teams purpose in considerations with others who are not part of the functioning team?

953. How do you manage human resources?

954. To what degree do all members feel responsible for all agreed-upon measures?

955. Can familiarity breed backup?

956. If you have criticized someones work for method variance in your role as reviewer, what was the circumstance?

957. What makes opportunities more or less obvious?

958. What are you doing specifically to develop the leaders around you?

959. To what degree do members articulate the goals beyond the team membership?

960. When a reviewer complains about method variance, what is the essence of the complaint?

961. Social categorization and intergroup behaviour: Does minimal intergroup discrimination make social identity more positive?

3.9 Team Member Performance Assessment: Loyalty Program

962. What is the large, desired outcome?

963. How do you work together to improve teaching and learning?

964. How do you implement Cost Reduction?

965. To what degree do the goals specify concrete team work products?

966. To what degree is there a sense that only the team can succeed?

967. Does statute or regulation require the job responsibility?

968. What happens if a team member receives a Rating of Unsatisfactory?

969. How often should assessments be conducted?

970. What are the staffs preferences for training on technology-based platforms?

971. Does the rater (supervisor) have to wait for the interim or final performance assessment review to tell an employee that the employees performance is unsatisfactory?

972. What steps have you taken to improve

performance?

973. To what degree does the teams approach to its work allow for modification and improvement over time?

974. How should adaptive assessments be implemented?

975. How are evaluation results utilized?

976. What qualities does a successful Team leader possess?

977. How often are assessments to be conducted?

978. What makes them effective?

979. Do the goals support your organizations goals?

3.10 Issue Log: Loyalty Program

980. Which stakeholders are thought leaders, influences, or early adopters?

981. Which stakeholders can influence others?

982. Are the stakeholders getting the information they need, are they consulted, are concerns addressed?

983. What are the typical contents?

984. Who reported the issue?

985. What is the stakeholders political influence?

986. Do you often overlook a key stakeholder or stakeholder group?

987. What would have to change?

988. Who have you worked with in past, similar initiatives?

989. Who are the members of the governing body?

990. Are stakeholder roles recognized by your organization?

991. Who is the issue assigned to?

992. Do you feel more overwhelmed by stakeholders?

993. Where do team members get information?

994. Is the issue log kept in a safe place?

995. Is access to the Issue Log controlled?

4.0 Monitoring and Controlling Process Group: Loyalty Program

996. Is it what was agreed upon?

997. How many more potential communications channels were introduced by the discovery of the new stakeholders?

998. What do they need to know about the Loyalty Program project?

999. How do you monitor progress?

1000. What is the timeline?

1001. Propriety: who needs to be involved in the evaluation to be ethical?

1002. How well did you do?

1003. Are the services being delivered?

1004. Is the program in place as intended?

1005. Overall, how does the program function to serve the clients?

1006. How well did the team follow the chosen processes?

1007. What business situation is being addressed?

1008. Just how important is your work to the overall success of the Loyalty Program project?

1009. What resources are necessary?

1010. How well defined and documented were the Loyalty Program project management processes you chose to use?

1011. Did you implement the program as designed?

1012. How are you doing?

1013. Purpose: toward what end is the evaluation being conducted?

4.1 Project Performance Report: Loyalty Program

1014. What is in it for you?

1015. To what degree are the demands of the task compatible with and converge with the relationships of the informal organization?

1016. To what degree do team members frequently explore the teams purpose and its implications?

1017. To what degree is the team cognizant of small wins to be celebrated along the way?

1018. To what degree will the team adopt a concrete, clearly understood, and agreed-upon approach that will result in achievement of the teams goals?

1019. To what degree does the teams purpose contain themes that are particularly meaningful and memorable?

1020. To what degree is there centralized control of information sharing?

1021. To what degree does the teams work approach provide opportunity for members to engage in open interaction?

1022. To what degree are fresh input and perspectives systematically caught and added (for example, through information and analysis, new members, and senior sponsors)?

1023. To what degree does the formal organization make use of individual resources and meet individual needs?

1024. To what degree are the members clear on what they are individually responsible for and what they are jointly responsible for?

1025. To what degree does the teams purpose constitute a broader, deeper aspiration than just accomplishing short-term goals?

1026. To what degree are the teams goals and objectives clear, simple, and measurable?

1027. To what degree do team members feel that the purpose of the team is important, if not exciting?

1028. To what degree does the task meet individual needs?

4.2 Variance Analysis: Loyalty Program

1029. What business event causes fluctuations?

1030. What are the actual costs to date?

1031. What was the cause of the increase in costs?

1032. How does the monthly budget compare to the actual experience?

1033. When, during the last four quarters, did a primary business event occur causing a fluctuation?

1034. Are all elements of indirect expense identified to overhead cost budgets of Loyalty Program projections?

1035. Is there a logical explanation for any variance?

1036. Does the contractors system identify work accomplishment against the schedule plan?

1037. What is the incurrence of actual indirect costs in excess of budgets, by element of expense?

1038. Are significant decision points, constraints, and interfaces identified as key milestones?

1039. Who are responsible for the establishment of budgets and assignment of resources for overhead performance?

1040. Are material costs reported within the same period as that in which BCWP is earned for that material?

1041. How are material, labor, and overhead variances calculated and recorded?

1042. How does the use of a single conversion element (rather than the traditional labor and overhead elements) affect standard costing?

1043. Are records maintained to show how undistributed budgets are controlled?

1044. Are work packages assigned to performing organizations?

1045. What should management do?

4.3 Earned Value Status: Loyalty Program

1046. When is it going to finish?

1047. Are you hitting your Loyalty Program projects targets?

1048. Where is evidence-based earned value in your organization reported?

1049. Verification is a process of ensuring that the developed system satisfies the stakeholders agreements and specifications; Are you building the product right? What do you verify?

1050. If earned value management (EVM) is so good in determining the true status of a Loyalty Program project and Loyalty Program project its completion, why is it that hardly any one uses it in information systems related Loyalty Program projects?

1051. How much is it going to cost by the finish?

1052. How does this compare with other Loyalty Program projects?

1053. Earned value can be used in almost any Loyalty Program project situation and in almost any Loyalty Program project environment. it may be used on large Loyalty Program projects, medium sized Loyalty Program projects, tiny Loyalty Program projects (in cut-down form), complex and simple Loyalty Program projects and in any market sector. some people, of course, know all about earned value, they have used it for years - but perhaps not as effectively as they could have?

1054. Where are your problem areas?

1055. Validation is a process of ensuring that the developed system will actually achieve the stakeholders desired outcomes; Are you building the right product? What do you validate?

1056. What is the unit of forecast value?

4.4 Risk Audit: Loyalty Program

1057. Level of preparation and skill?

1058. How are risk appetites expressed?

1059. Does your auditor understand your business?

1060. Is Loyalty Program project scope stable?

1061. Does your board meet regularly and document all decisions and actions?

1062. Does your organization have a process for meeting its ongoing taxation obligations?

1063. What compliance systems do you have in place to address quality, errors, and outcomes?

1064. Are all programs planned and conducted according to recognized safety standards?

1065. Is all required equipment available?

1066. For paid staff, does your organization comply with the minimum conditions for employment and/or the applicable modern award?

1067. Have staff received necessary training?

1068. What is the anticipated volatility of the requirements?

1069. Does the customer have a solid idea of what is

required?

1070. Do you have written and signed agreements/contracts in place for each paid staff member?

1071. Do you have a procedure for dealing with complaints?

1072. Is the auditor able to evaluate contradictory evidence in an unbiased manner?

1073. Does your organization have a social media policy and procedure?

1074. Is there a screening process that will ensure all participants have the fitness and skills required to safely participate?

1075. Improving fraud detection: do auditors react to abnormal inconsistencies between financial and non-financial measures?

4.5 Contractor Status Report: Loyalty Program

1076. What is the average response time for answering a support call?

1077. Describe how often regular updates are made to the proposed solution. Are corresponding regular updates included in the standard maintenance plan?

1078. Who can list a Loyalty Program project as organization experience, your organization or a previous employee of your organization?

1079. What was the final actual cost?

1080. What process manages the contracts?

1081. What was the actual budget or estimated cost for your organizations services?

1082. How long have you been using the services?

1083. How is risk transferred?

1084. What are the minimum and optimal bandwidth requirements for the proposed solution?

1085. Are there contractual transfer concerns?

1086. If applicable; describe your standard schedule for new software version releases. Are new software version releases included in the standard maintenance plan?

1087. How does the proposed individual meet each requirement?

1088. What was the overall budget or estimated cost?

1089. What was the budget or estimated cost for your organizations services?

4.6 Formal Acceptance: Loyalty Program

1090. What function(s) does it fill or meet?

1091. Do you buy pre-configured systems or build your own configuration?

1092. Was the sponsor/customer satisfied?

1093. What is the Acceptance Management Process?

1094. Does it do what Loyalty Program project team said it would?

1095. Do you perform formal acceptance or burn-in tests?

1096. What features, practices, and processes proved to be strengths or weaknesses?

1097. General estimate of the costs and times to complete the Loyalty Program project?

1098. How does your team plan to obtain formal acceptance on your Loyalty Program project?

1099. What are the requirements against which to test, Who will execute?

1100. Is formal acceptance of the Loyalty Program project product documented and distributed?

1101. Was business value realized?

1102. Was the Loyalty Program project goal achieved?

1103. Was the Loyalty Program project work done on time, within budget, and according to specification?

1104. How well did the team follow the methodology?

1105. Was the client satisfied with the Loyalty Program project results?

1106. Did the Loyalty Program project manager and team act in a professional and ethical manner?

1107. Does it do what client said it would?

1108. Have all comments been addressed?

1109. What lessons were learned about your Loyalty Program project management methodology?

5.0 Closing Process Group: Loyalty Program

1110. Was the user/client satisfied with the end product?

1111. What areas does the group agree are the biggest success on the Loyalty Program project?

1112. What was learned?

1113. What level of risk does the proposed budget represent to the Loyalty Program project?

1114. What is the overall risk of the Loyalty Program project to your organization?

1115. Is the Loyalty Program project funded?

1116. Did you do things well?

1117. Did the Loyalty Program project team have the right skills?

1118. How critical is the Loyalty Program project success to the success of your organization?

1119. Will the Loyalty Program project deliverable(s) replace a current asset or group of assets?

1120. How dependent is the Loyalty Program project on other Loyalty Program projects or work efforts?

1121. Who are the Loyalty Program project stakeholders?

1122. What can you do better next time, and what specific actions can you take to improve?

5.1 Procurement Audit: Loyalty Program

1123. Are there mechanisms for evaluating the departments suppliers performance in relation to prices, quality, delivery and innovation?

1124. Does the cash disbursement policy prohibit drawing checks to cash or bearer?

1125. Is the chosen supplier part of your organizations database?

1126. Are vendor price lists regularly updated?

1127. Are there systems for recording and managing stocks (where part of contract)?

1128. Is the functioning of automatic disbursement programs tested by an independent party?

1129. Does the individual approving disbursements sign or initial the document?

1130. Audits: when was your last independent public accountant (ipa) audit and what were the results?

1131. Are outsourcing and Public Private Partnerships considered as alternatives to in-house work?

1132. Were results of the award procedures published?

1133. Did you consider and evaluate alternatives, like bundling needs with other departments or grouping supplies in separate lots with different characteristics?

1134. Is free and fair (international) competition promoted by organizational policies and legislation, in line with legal, trade organizations and other policies?

1135. Are proper financing arrangements taken?

1136. How do you ensure whether the goods were supplied or works executed in time and properly recorded in measurement books and stock/works registers after inspection?

1137. Is there any objection?

1138. Is the minutes book kept current?

1139. When tenders were actually rejected because they were abnormally low, were reasons for this decision given and were they sufficiently grounded?

1140. Did the contracting authority draw up a comprehensive written report about progress and outcome of the procurement process?

1141. Does the procurement Loyalty Program project have a clear goal and does the goal meet the specified needs of the users?

5.2 Contract Close-Out: Loyalty Program

1142. What is capture management?

1143. Parties: who is involved?

1144. Was the contract type appropriate?

1145. Change in circumstances?

1146. Are the signers the authorized officials?

1147. What happens to the recipient of services?

1148. How/when used ?

1149. How does it work?

1150. Have all acceptance criteria been met prior to final payment to contractors?

1151. Parties: Authorized?

1152. Change in attitude or behavior?

1153. Has each contract been audited to verify acceptance and delivery?

1154. Have all contract records been included in the Loyalty Program project archives?

1155. Was the contract sufficiently clear so as not to

result in numerous disputes and misunderstandings?

1156. Change in knowledge?

1157. Have all contracts been completed?

1158. Have all contracts been closed?

1159. Was the contract complete without requiring numerous changes and revisions?

1160. How is the contracting office notified of the automatic contract close-out?

5.3 Project or Phase Close-Out: Loyalty Program

1161. Which changes might a stakeholder be required to make as a result of the Loyalty Program project?

1162. How often did each stakeholder need an update?

1163. Have business partners been involved extensively, and what data was required for them?

1164. What could be done to improve the process?

1165. In preparing the Lessons Learned report, should it reflect a consensus viewpoint, or should the report reflect the different individual viewpoints?

1166. What were the desired outcomes?

1167. Planned completion date?

1168. What were the goals and objectives of the communications strategy for the Loyalty Program project?

1169. Planned remaining costs?

1170. Was the schedule met?

1171. If you were the Loyalty Program project sponsor, how would you determine which Loyalty Program project team(s) and/or individuals deserve recognition?

1172. What are the informational communication needs for each stakeholder?

1173. What information did each stakeholder need to contribute to the Loyalty Program projects success?

1174. Who controlled key decisions that were made?

1175. What stakeholder group needs, expectations, and interests are being met by the Loyalty Program project?

1176. What benefits or impacts does the stakeholder group expect to obtain as a result of the Loyalty Program project?

1177. What advantages do the an individual interview have over a group meeting, and vice-versa?

1178. What was expected from each stakeholder?

1179. Does the lesson educate others to improve performance?

1180. What is a Risk Management Process?

5.4 Lessons Learned: Loyalty Program

1181. How effective was Loyalty Program project Team member training?

1182. What were the lessons learned on this Loyalty Program project?

1183. How adequately involved did you feel in Loyalty Program project decisions?

1184. What were the challenges and pitfalls?

1185. How effective was the documentation that you received with the Loyalty Program project product/service?

1186. How effective were Best Practices & Lessons Learned from prior Loyalty Program projects utilized in this Loyalty Program project?

1187. Overall, how effective was the performance of the Loyalty Program project Manager?

1188. How effective were the techniques used to prepare you and your organization for the impact of the changes brought about by the product or service produced by the Loyalty Program project?

1189. How effective was the quality assurance process?

1190. What is the supplier dependency?

1191. Overall, how effective were the efforts to prepare you and your organization for the impact of the product/service of the Loyalty Program project?

1192. Was the purpose of the Loyalty Program project, the end products and success criteria clearly defined and agreed at the start?

1193. Who is responsible for each action?

1194. How well does the product or service the Loyalty Program project produced meet your needs?

1195. Do you conduct the engineering tests?

1196. How well prepared were you to receive Loyalty Program project deliverables?

1197. Are lessons learned documented?

1198. How useful and complete was the Loyalty Program project document repository?

1199. What are the skills directly related to the task?

Index

affect 100, 104, 111, 114, 137, 147, 171, 201, 221, 223-224, 235, 266, 277, 283, 286, 342, 360, 370, 381
affected   39, 135-136, 177-178, 197, 221, 278, 334, 359
affecting   15
affects 172
affinity 38
afford 123, 199, 336
afraid 192
against26, 211, 236, 252, 256-257, 365, 370, 380, 388
agencies   343
agenda   233, 248, 266
agents 28, 189
aggregate   40
agreed   39, 41, 143, 177-178, 214, 280, 376, 399
Agreement   5, 9, 144, 232, 368
agreements   213, 246, 248, 257, 382, 385
agrees 326
airline 28, 96
alerting   143, 280
algorithms   204, 342
aligned   22, 126, 228
Alignment   346
alleged   1
alliance   38
alliances   39
allocate   293, 316
allocated   192, 245, 263
allocating   191, 293
allocation   228
allowance   142, 277
allowances   233, 368
allowed   169, 364
allows 13, 303
almost 71, 246, 382
already   77, 82, 87, 91, 101, 114, 155, 171, 220, 254, 292-293, 308, 324, 356
Although   130
altogether   343
always 13, 70, 72
ambitious   236, 370
amended   151
amount   98, 257, 288
amounts   231

411

engagement 36, 69, 73, 107, 126, 134, 233, 270, 334, 365
engaging   50
enhance   122, 125, 249
enough   11, 32, 47, 75, 79, 85, 116, 119, 122, 144, 147, 255, 263, 266, 278, 283
enroll 23, 79, 83, 85
enrolled   76, 81, 110
ensure 26, 47, 58, 151, 185, 187, 189, 195, 210, 218, 222, 230, 232, 234, 240, 243, 248, 257, 277, 308, 323, 326, 330, 347, 366, 368, 385, 393
ensuring   13, 246-247, 382-383
Enterprise 121, 220, 357
enthusiast 101
entire 176, 187, 293, 312, 340
entities 140, 227, 364
entity 1, 23, 281
entrance   228
envisaged   137
equipment   130, 233, 249, 351, 354, 368, 384
equipped   25
equitably   30, 234
equivalent 315
errors 186, 288, 293, 384
escalated   254, 316
Escalation 314
especially 308
essence   371
essential   234
establish   52, 124, 181, 199, 319
estimate   140, 173, 179-180, 253, 294, 310, 316, 348, 388
-estimate   178, 314
estimated   30, 32, 93, 140-141, 177, 181, 201, 211, 250, 318-319, 386-387
estimates   3-4, 7, 31, 45, 140, 142, 155, 171, 179, 183, 195, 244-245, 292, 308, 316, 321
Estimating 3-4, 7, 142, 173, 181-182, 295, 310, 318-319
estimation 137, 213, 346
estimator   180, 316
ethical 252, 376, 389
ethics 340
evaluate   52, 211, 214, 244, 256, 286, 328, 343, 385, 393
evaluated   55, 257
evaluating 57, 392

impact4, 8, 30, 36, 38-42, 59, 130, 138, 144, 172, 183-184, 203, 205, 223, 237, 244, 309, 321, 328, 336, 338, 340, 342, 352-353, 360, 370, 398-399

impacted   267, 286-288

impacting   176

impacts   137, 174, 200, 271, 287, 310, 397

implement   60, 71, 84, 95, 117, 359, 372, 377

importance   234, 243, 348, 370

important   20, 61, 76, 79, 84, 101, 105, 110, 132, 138, 197, 215, 217, 236, 242, 248, 254, 274, 279, 334, 346, 350, 354, 377, 379

improve   2, 13, 40, 42, 46, 49-50, 52, 55, 57-58, 61, 77, 169, 188, 217, 254, 261-262, 266, 268, 306, 322, 332, 372, 391, 396-397

improved   57-58, 66, 212, 262

improving   54, 63, 220, 357, 385

inaccurate   143

inactive   179, 316

inactivity   116

incentive   50, 75, 119

incentives   64, 76, 113

inception   118

incident   202, 226, 363

incidents   99

include   72, 144, 210, 245, 276, 292, 348

included   2, 11, 51, 145, 150, 173, 181, 187, 217, 222, 250, 259, 285, 289, 310-311, 318, 358, 386, 394

includes   13, 42

including   24, 26, 32, 53, 155, 236, 238, 245, 287

incomplete   143

increase   72, 74, 77, 95, 104, 115-116, 120, 186, 213, 289, 380

increased   69, 73

increasing   41, 226, 363

incurrence   380

in-depth   12, 14

indicate   38, 61, 364

indicated   63

indicators   100, 137, 155, 185, 205, 227, 329, 340

indirect   191, 245, 292-293, 316-317, 328, 380

indirectly   1, 64

individual   1, 174, 193, 210, 242, 250, 256, 262, 277, 296, 368, 379, 387, 392, 396-397

industrial   341-342

maintain   60, 108, 117, 142, 257
maintained   155, 191, 365, 381
majors 117
makers 209, 267
making   56, 100, 190, 201, 236, 241, 273, 326, 331, 355
manage   53, 55, 97, 130-132, 135-136, 139, 142, 147, 175,
185, 199, 214, 238, 248, 257, 263, 272, 275, 283, 288, 298, 312,
314, 326, 334, 343, 371
manageable 33, 195, 308, 332
managed   11, 126, 209, 253, 314
management 1, 3-8, 12-13, 19, 21, 26, 28, 32, 49, 53, 56-57, 92,
110, 130, 135, 139-141, 143, 149-152, 157-158, 172-173, 175-177,
179, 183-185, 189, 191, 195, 197, 199-203, 205, 209-210, 213, 215,
217-218, 220, 226, 230, 241, 246, 248-249, 253-254, 260, 262, 264,
267, 271, 275-279, 285-286, 288, 292, 294-295, 298, 306, 308, 311-
314, 316, 320-322, 326-327, 332, 334, 336-337, 339-340, 346-347,
350, 352, 355-357, 362, 365, 367, 377, 381-382, 388-389, 394, 397
manager   11, 13, 26, 32, 130, 142-143, 179, 185, 209, 213,
219, 252, 280, 285, 328, 347, 356, 389, 398
managers   2, 6, 56, 129, 139, 199, 218, 265, 309, 332, 337
manages   250, 268, 386
managing   2, 6, 129, 134, 265, 267, 270, 279, 365, 392
mandate   268
mandatory   223, 360
manner   102, 151, 155, 191, 218, 240, 244-245, 252, 329,
358-359, 385, 389
Manual   152, 365
mapped   30
mapping   217
margin 93
marginal   101
marked   286
market 21, 57, 72, 77, 87, 93, 118, 122, 163, 199, 211, 234, 246,
300, 383
marketable   199
marketer   11
marketers   50
marketing   22, 38, 40-41, 43, 46, 50, 55-56, 62, 66, 73, 75, 77,
79, 82, 91, 95, 102-104, 110-112, 117, 121, 151, 163, 272, 281
mascot   108
material   132, 191-192, 212, 381
materials   1, 233
matrices   147, 283

provided   15, 63, 151, 195-196, 209-212, 233, 278, 347-348, 368
provider   23, 46, 58, 69, 91
providers   28
provides   164, 170, 210, 307
providing   134, 150, 270, 285, 301, 312
provision   363
provisions   27
public 80-81, 137, 392
published   211, 256, 392
publisher   1
purchase   11, 21, 56-57, 68, 73, 77, 84, 86, 91, 97, 100, 105, 118, 256, 348, 354
purchases   41, 116, 213
purchasing   58, 103
purpose   2, 13, 105, 132, 182, 240, 242-243, 306-307, 313, 319, 362, 371, 377-379, 399
purposes   156
qualified   30, 157, 257, 275, 285, 294
qualities   81, 373
quality 1, 4-5, 7, 9, 13, 40, 42, 44, 46-47, 50, 62, 65, 77, 92, 131, 137, 141-142, 157, 171-172, 185, 187-189, 193, 195-196, 209, 217-218, 222, 226-228, 240, 257, 267, 274, 278, 315, 322, 324, 326-327, 331-332, 346, 350, 354, 358, 362, 364-365, 384, 392, 398
quantify   40
quantity   212
quarters   380
question   14, 19, 24, 35, 44, 52, 60, 68, 190
questions   11-12, 14, 108, 174, 198, 217, 310
quickly 13, 179, 337
quotes 211
raised 286
rarely 76
rather 249, 381
rating 212, 348, 372
ratings 349
rational   245, 329
rationale   277
reached   102
reaching   83
readiness   294
reading   111
readings   65

reported   56, 150, 191, 195, 246, 350, 374, 381-382
reporting   65, 156, 192, 202, 249, 279, 309, 322
reports 92, 99, 134, 139, 150, 178, 180, 195, 209, 270, 315, 332
repository   399
represent   216, 223-224, 360, 390
reproduced   1
repurchase   92
request   5, 8, 143-144, 221-224, 280, 320, 358, 360-361
requested   1, 211, 224, 349, 359, 361
requests   221, 348, 358-359
require 29, 32, 132, 167, 204, 268, 292, 304, 312, 342, 372
required   32-33, 38, 130-131, 145, 160-162, 170, 195, 198,
201, 205, 210, 215, 227-228, 240, 261-263, 267, 272, 277, 292, 296-
297, 299, 310, 316, 324, 326, 334, 346, 352-354, 364, 368, 384-385,
396
requires   130, 212
requiring   134, 259, 270, 395
research   47, 228
reserve 180, 292
reserved   1
reserves   141, 191, 277
reside 83, 369
resistance   352
resolution   155, 232
resolve 230, 299, 366, 369
resolved   176, 232, 239, 254, 316, 336
resource   3-4, 7-8, 137, 158, 161, 167, 169-170, 195, 200,
210, 220, 228, 299, 304, 306-307, 332, 346, 356
resources   2, 11, 25, 33, 46, 53, 64, 69, 114, 130, 132, 135,
137, 146, 150-151, 161, 166, 169-170, 174, 181, 195-196, 210, 233,
245, 277, 282, 285, 292, 294, 296, 298-299, 307, 312, 318, 320,
347, 368, 371, 377, 379-380
respect   1, 74
respond   122, 138, 192, 352
responded   15
responding   99
response   60-63, 250, 352, 386
responses   342
responsive   173, 182, 319
restaurant   68, 98, 113
result   49, 53, 181, 183, 197, 216, 224, 260, 262, 286, 319, 334,
352, 361, 378, 395-397
resulted   61

started 12, 163, 166
starting 13
startup 132
start-up   95, 367
stated 82, 87, 101, 155, 171, 255, 292-293, 308, 324
statement   3, 6, 14, 141, 149-151, 171, 217, 285, 287-288, 317
statements   15, 23, 29, 32, 34, 43, 50-51, 59, 67, 127, 190
statistics   178, 286
status 5-6, 8-9, 42, 77, 79, 102, 109, 111, 123, 150, 155, 195, 209,
219, 221, 230, 238, 246, 250, 279, 314-315, 329, 332, 350, 356,
359, 366, 382, 386
statute 372
statutory   32, 231, 366
Steering   209
stocks 392
stopper   146
storage   222
stored 45, 107, 144
stores 84, 93, 103
storing 48
strategic   78, 133, 196, 249, 338, 346
strategies   41, 75, 149, 175, 200, 225-226, 286-287, 337, 353,
362-363, 365
strategy   22, 28, 78-79, 84, 92, 104, 112, 137, 152, 185, 201,
217, 226, 273-274, 288, 335, 337, 350, 362, 396
strength   227, 365
strengths   48, 73, 158, 163-164, 252, 272, 295, 368, 388
strive   218
strong 248, 330
Strongly   14, 19, 24, 35, 44, 52, 60, 68
structural   370
structure   3, 7, 23, 53-55, 113, 123, 153-154, 169, 210, 215,
277, 290-291, 306, 352
structured   112, 195, 332
structures   137, 156, 242-243, 274
styles   322
subdivide   155
subdivided   156, 328
subfactor   348
subject 12-13, 29, 279
Subjective   187, 324
submitted   223, 360
subsequent   211

CPSIA information can be obtained
at www.ICGtesting.com
Printed in the USA
BVHW041912130919
558404BV00016B/130/P